# Evolving *You*

Nine enduring principles
for lasting leadership growth

Dr. Samantha Madhosingh

First published in Great Britain by Practical Inspiration Publishing, 2024

ISBN   9781788605823      (hardback)
       9781788605373      (paperback)
       9781788605397      (epub)
       9781788605380      (mobi)

Want to bulk-buy copies of this book for your team and colleagues? We can customize the content and co-brand *Evolving You* to suit your business's needs.

Please email info@practicalinspiration.com for more details.

# Praise for *Evolving You*

A truly excellent book from Dr. Samantha Madhosingh. I have read a great many books on leadership from many so-called gurus and academics on the subject. But never have I read one which uses simple to understand language and provides an easy-to-follow structure that does not pre-suppose long leadership experience, and one that really resonated in terms of how-to and useful resources. I absolutely loved it and will use its content to challenge my own long-held views on great leadership.

Rachid "Ben" Bengougam, Senior Vice President HR, Hilton

This book will transform the way you lead, evolving you into an effective and compassionate leader who can inspire others towards action.

Simon Alexander Ong, bestselling author of *Energize*, international Keynote Speaker and award-winning Coach

Dr. Samantha's book is compelling. I love that it contains practical, simple but effective tools to enable readers to make change for themselves. Unlike some "self-help" books, Dr. Samantha neither patronizes the reader nor leaves them alone to figure it all out. It's clear that her personal journey as a high-achiever has informed this book, and if people can walk her path, then success is the likely outcome.

Professor John Amaechi OBE, New York Times bestselling author

With profound insights and practical wisdom, this book masterfully intertwines the crucial aspects of self-discovery and emotional intelligence with the practicalities of relationship mastery and resilience. Dr. Madhosingh's approach transcends conventional leadership narratives, urging readers to embark on a transformative journey of personal growth and relational skill-building. Whether you're a seasoned leader or just beginning your leadership journey, this book offers a refreshing and comprehensive roadmap to achieve lasting leadership growth and make a significant impact in both personal and professional spheres.

Mark Murphy, New York Times bestselling author and Founder of Leadership IQ

A must-read for anyone in leadership. Dr. Samantha provides truly valuable insights, leadership lessons and tools that will help to transform anyone looking to get to the next level of effective and inspirational leadership. A book that every leader should have on their desk.

Julie Ennis, MBA, Executive, CBRE

Dr. Samantha Madhosingh's book on leadership is nothing short of transformative. A truly indispensable resource for anyone aspiring to elevate their leadership skills. In a saturated market of leadership literature, her work stands out as truly excellent. This book goes beyond theory; it's a practical guide equipped with simple yet effective tools that empower readers to instigate meaningful change. As a global director myself, I am committed to using the book's content to challenge and evolve my long-held views on what great leadership is. *Evolving You* is a beacon for those seeking to become effective and compassionate leaders, capable of inspiring others toward meaningful action.

Amit Sirker, Global Director of Renewal Operations—SaaS Company

*Evolving You* is outstanding and the timing for this book couldn't be better. Dr. Samantha Madhosingh's leadership insights are invaluable!

Kym Yancey, President & Chief Marketing Officer, eWomenNetwork

What an easy read! Dr. Samantha gently weans you from your lifelong limiting beliefs and shows how, through communication and resilience, your inner leadership qualities will naturally emerge.

Brian Smith, UGG Founder

I just had the pleasure of reading Dr. Samantha Madhosingh's book, *Evolving You*. Dr. Madhosingh takes the reader through a journey of exploration into themselves, finding what is blocking them from achieving their full potential. She guides you through understanding yourself and others, then takes you on a guided tour of how sustainable growth can be achieved. This book is ideal for any leader who feels stuck, or in the process of moving to a new paradigm. Excellent addition to the body of knowledge.

Dr. Betty® Uribe, CEO, Effectus Enterprises, dba Dr. Betty®, Board Director, Entrepreneur, Business Advisor, Investor, Philanthropist, Global Influencer, UN Ambassador for Peace and Human Rights (UNICEF, UN, OEA, CNDH, CDIH, UNESCO)

In *Evolving You: Nine enduring principles for lasting leadership growth*, the focus on foundational growth resonates with my ethos of nurturing inclusive, engaged leaders. The book's emphasis on "Building Inner Leadership" through self-awareness and emotional regulation is a cornerstone for effective leadership. It underscores the importance of understanding oneself as a prelude to leading others.

"Relationship Mastery," which champions the power of connections and social skills, aligns with my belief in creating cohesive, inclusive teams. The concept of "Cultivating the Whole Leader" stresses personal resilience, a vital aspect of sustainable leadership encompassing more than technical skills.

Overall, the book serves as a practical guide, offering a transformative journey from self-mastery to relational skills and resilience, essential for leaders driving innovation and adapting to change.

Dr. Rachel Talton, CEO and
Founder Synergy International Limited, Inc.

I highly recommend this book: *Evolving You: Nine enduring principles for lasting leadership growth.* My recommendation stems solely from the fact that we are witnessing shifts in management and leadership skills that are sorely needed to navigate the "new normal" of business, spirituality, and relationships. The practical steps outlined in this book grounds us in both reality and humility. As a leader in a large public university, I appreciate her insights from a psychological perspective because we are always task oriented, and at times we forget to pause long enough to see if we are being effective and efficient. A great book to provide us some tools to augment what we already know.

Gerald L. Hector, CPA, Author and
Executive in Higher Education

*To my wonderful daughter, Sofia*

*In your eyes, I see the limitless potential of tomorrow and the joyful curiosity that lights the path of discovery. Your adventurous spirit and unwavering zest for life inspire me each day to keep evolving. Since the moment you were born, you are my reason for everything.*

# Contents

*Introduction*                                                            *xi*

**PART 1: FOUNDATIONS OF THE SELF:**
**BUILDING INNER LEADERSHIP**                                              **1**

1   Self-Discovery: Laying the Foundations of
    Awareness and Control                                                   3
2   Rewriting the Script: The Unlearning
    Process of Self-Discovery and Growth                                   29
3   Stay the Course: The Power of Commitment
    and Consistency                                                        47

**PART 2: RELATIONSHIP MASTERY:**
**CULTIVATING THE SKILLS OF CONNECTION**                                  **69**

4   Understanding Others: Mastering Social
    Awareness and Relationship Management                                  71
5   Beyond Words: The Nuances of
    Powerful Communication                                                 91
6   Compassionate Command: Leading with
    Heart and Understanding                                               117

**PART 3: CULTIVATING THE WHOLE LEADER:**
**EMBRACING PERSONAL RENEWAL**
**AND COLLECTIVE STRENGTH**                                              **135**

7   Sustained Growth: Renew, Recharge,
    and Refuel for the Journey Ahead                                      137
8   Your Support System: Finding Strength
    in Community                                                          155
9   Standing Strong: Harnessing Resilience
    in Leadership's Toughest Moments                                      171

*Conclusion*                          *185*

*Notes*                               *187*

*Exercises*                           *191*

*Emotion Vocabulary*                  *197*

*Acknowledgments*                     *199*

*About the Author*                    *201*

*Index*                               *203*

# Introduction

*The greatest leaders mobilize others by coalescing people around a shared vision.*

KENNETH H. BLANCHARD

Many people don't realize they're already leaders. But they are. Through their actions, even if they aren't already in a management or senior leadership role, they inspire others and contribute to their growth. Leadership is not just about your job title. And if you are in a leadership role, developing yourself is essential. It goes beyond mastering a specific course or following an inflexible management style. To be an exceptional leader, you must dedicate yourself to a continuous process of self-discovery, refinement, and adaptation. Leaders committed to their own evolution are better equipped to inspire their team, drive innovation, adapt to change, and drive sustainable success.

True evolution is a multidimensional process, demanding more than just technical skills or a by-the-book approach to management. It's an unfolding journey of increasing self-awareness, sharpened emotional intelligence, and the kind of adaptability that meets change head-on.

My own evolution has been fueled by a relentless curiosity about who I am and what I believe. This journey led me to confront the fears, biases, and limiting beliefs holding me back. I've applied the principles discussed in this book to continually refine my thought patterns, beliefs, and communication skills. I use the same transformative approach in my work with leaders and organizations, helping them uncover and address deep-seated narratives that hinder their growth. Whether you need to improve communication, set healthier boundaries, or enhance productivity, this book can be your guide.

This book isn't about hard skills, the technical competencies that many believe form the basis of leadership. No, it's about the often-neglected soft skills: emotional intelligence, teamwork, communication, and problem-solving, to name a few. These skills should consume the lion's share of any training budget, but they generally don't—despite being the real keys to leadership success.

Many leaders often find themselves in leadership roles without being shown how to excel, so it's important to understand this: your commitment to personal growth has far-reaching implications—on your team, organization, and career trajectory.

This book will help you be a better leader and guide you through a reflective process, showing how your internal leadership can profoundly influence the external world. Each principle will take you on a transformative journey, beginning with the crucial underpinnings of self and inner leadership and culminating in advanced relational skills and resilience. The core message is simple: your evolution as an individual directly contributes to your effectiveness as a leader. A dedicated focus on your growth elevates your leadership capabilities and empowers you to lead, guide, and inspire more effectively.

The first part of the book, "Foundations of the Self: Building Inner Leadership," lays the groundwork for your self-discovery. Chapter 1 offers a structured approach to cultivating self-awareness and managing emotions and behaviors. You will explore your outdated thoughts and beliefs to better understand who you are at your core and how this drives your actions and impacts your life. Chapter 2 expands this self-exploration by uncovering the "scripts" or preset notions developed during the formative years, examining their long-lasting impact on our adult lives and professional roles. Because these scripts don't just fade away, they continue to exert a subtle yet profound influence on our daily interactions and decision-making processes. In Chapter 3, we continue the conversation to focus on staying the course through commitment and consistency. This chapter underscores the importance of making and fulfilling goals, serving as a basis for building integrity.

For the second part of this book, "Relationship Mastery: Cultivating the Skills of Connection," we turn the lens from the inner self to the world outside. This section of the book is designed to arm leaders with the relational skills they often overlook yet desperately need. Chapter 4 delves into the art and science of social awareness, guiding you through the maze of social cues and subtexts that make up interpersonal relationships. Chapter 5 expands this dialogue by providing a comprehensive toolkit for effective communication. It explores what to say, how to say it, and, perhaps most importantly, how to interpret nonverbal messages and listen effectively. Chapter 6 explains how important it is for leaders to lead with heart and understanding. We closely examine what empathy is and offer guidelines for how to cultivate it.

And, finally, the last part of this book, "Cultivating the Whole Leader: Embracing Personal Renewal and Collective Strength," explores all the facets of taking care of yourself so that you can be present for others. It delves into holistic well-being as a pillar of sustainable leadership. Chapter 7 is a crucial reminder of the many facets of self-care, underscoring that neglecting yourself is a pitfall all leaders should avoid. Dismissing this chapter as irrelevant would be a strategic mistake, for self-care isn't a luxury but a necessity. Chapter 8 delves deeper into the importance of building and maintaining a robust support system. Here, you'll discover why a nurturing community isn't just a nice-to-have but a foundational element for your sustained growth. Finally, Chapter 9 prepares you for the harsher realities of leadership. It provides you with an arsenal of strategies to develop resilience, which will be your ally in navigating the unavoidable challenges and hurdles that come with being a leader. This resilience is a long-term strategy that contributes to career longevity and effectiveness.

At the back of the book are some exercises you can do to help maximize your growth (pp. 189–94). They will be referenced in the chapters in Part 1.

I've often observed that articulating emotions is a challenge for many individuals. This difficulty is not due to a lack of feeling but instead is caused by a limited vocabulary to express these complex emotions. To bridge this gap, I have included an Emotion Vocabulary section at the back of this book (pp. 195–6). This section is not intended to be exhaustive, but provides a range of words that can help to describe your emotional state more accurately and richly. The aim is to empower readers with a broader linguistic base, enhancing their ability to communicate their feelings effectively and cultivating a deeper understanding of their emotional landscape.

I hope you will read this book all the way through at least once. And then revisit it again and again, each time you encounter new challenges or opportunities for reflection. It is here for you to use to help you develop and keep growing. Use it as a toolkit to fuel your ongoing evolution, continuously expand, and elevate yourself to new levels. And, most of all, use this book to help yourself, your colleagues, your team, and your organization to flourish and thrive.

* Please note that I've included some stories throughout the chapters to bring to life the principles I have outlined. They are all drawn from the real experiences of my clients, but to protect their anonymity I have changed names and some key details.

# PART 1

# Foundations of the Self: Building Inner Leadership

# 1

# Self-Discovery: Laying the Foundations of Awareness and Control

*I think self-awareness is probably the most important thing towards being a champion.*

BILLIE JEAN KING

A business is only as strong as its people.

As you embark on your journey to becoming a great leader, the first person you need to get to know intimately is yourself. Think about it—if you're going to guide a team, make big decisions, and navigate challenges, you've got to be sure of who you are, what you stand for, and where your weak spots lie. Knowing yourself inside and out will give you a solid base for evolving as a leader.

Self-discovery isn't about navel-gazing or getting lost deep in your thoughts. It's about being honest with yourself. It's recognizing when you're on your A-game and when you might be the one dropping the ball. It's about knowing what drives you, what scares you, and what inspires you to do better.

Once you've become interested in digging deeper and understanding yourself, the next step is developing your self-awareness. Self-awareness is *how* you discover more about yourself. It's the foundation of everything. The better you know yourself and your blind spots, the better equipped you'll be to catch yourself before a misstep or know when to double down on what you're good at.

Self-awareness is crucial to the development of an individual's character, and it's impossible to work on anything else until you discover and begin to master this skill. It is an essential mental muscle we must develop to make better decisions, communicate more effectively, and build stronger relationships. It comes from an internal reflection where we are able to clearly know our own values, passions, goals, triggers, reactions to things and situations (including our thoughts, beliefs, feelings, behaviors, strengths, and weaknesses), and the impact we have on others.

In my experience, the very best leaders are highly self-aware. It's a lot like building a house; if you don't have a solid, secure base, it will collapse with the slightest gust of wind. Self-awareness is the solid foundation, the base upon which everything else must be built.

And it is important to understand that there isn't a single destination you will arrive at, but an ongoing journey of exploration, offering new insights and understandings with each step. As leaders explore deeper into the nuances of their character, beliefs, and behaviors, they are better equipped to navigate the complexities of leadership with grace, agility, and authenticity.

If you're wondering whether or not you are generally self-aware, look at the statements below and see how many, if any, apply to you.

- You can observe and understand your emotions.
- You are curious about how you think, what you believe, and how you behave.
- You notice the impact of your behavior on others and care about it.
- You know and can acknowledge when you have made a mistake or hurt someone's feelings unintentionally.
- You know your ideals, passions, and core values. These shape everything you do.
- You are interested in knowing more about your shortcomings and what you can work on and use this information to grow and develop your skills.

- You pay attention to your strengths and challenges in every aspect of your life.

Remember, it's a rarity for any of us to be on-point with our self-awareness every single moment of every single day. There will be times when we're more in tune and curious than others. Some insights we have about ourselves might hit the mark, while others remain unexplored. And that's totally fine. After all, refining this skill is an ongoing journey.

# HOW YOUR THOUGHTS DIRECT YOUR LIFE

## Thoughts Feelings Actions Results

How often do you reflect on the "how" and "why" of your thoughts and actions? My guess is, probably not a lot. Most people are so caught up in the busy-ness of life to pause, reflect, and take stock of what is going on in their mind. Life is busy, I know. We're overworked, we're stressed, we always have something that needs to be done. Rarely do we observe things slowly, as they happen. Or wonder to ourselves, "Why am I feeling like this?"

Through self-awareness, we learn the ability to see ourselves more objectively—but it takes curiosity, reflection, and introspection.

The graphic above is a great tool you can use to identify what is really going on. I honestly don't remember where I exactly learned this, but it has been a great resource I use with many of my clients. It highlights that your thoughts and beliefs trigger your emotions, your emotions then trigger your actions and inactions; and your actions and inactions cause your results. More often than not, when we do this exercise together, we don't start at the beginning with *thoughts*, because much of the time the thoughts are just beyond their awareness. When I ask them what the thoughts are, they often tell me a feeling. What many people notice first is either how they are feeling or what actions they are or are not taking. So that is where we begin.

Here's the exercise:

> Take out a sheet of paper.
> Create four large columns (see the completed example on page 8).
> Across the top of each column write:
>
> THOUGHTS | FEELINGS | ACTIONS | RESULTS

Pick the column where you have some information you want to explore. This is the column you start in.

For example, let's say you have stayed in a dead-end role at work for several years and there have been multiple opportunities for promotion to a leadership position, but you have chosen in each instance not to apply. You're convinced they will not promote you, so think to yourself, "Why bother?"

Let's take a look at what that would look like if you were to write it all down. The key is to approach the exercise with curiosity. The goal is to discover what is at the root of you not applying for promotions and staying in a role you don't enjoy.

So, you'd write: "Stuck in the same dead-end role for years" in the RESULTS column.

Then go backwards. Ask yourself: "What actions am I taking or *not* taking that are giving me this result?" Write down your answers in the ACTIONS column. For this example, we have: "Not applying for a promotion" and "Not taking initiative in current job role."

The next step can be a bit tricky because it's about your feelings.

It's really important to separate what you think from what you feel. The reason this is tricky is because in our common use of language we often say "I feel" to mean "I think," and so many people confuse their thoughts with their feelings. Language is so important and understanding how to properly identify your thoughts from your feelings and keeping them clearly separate is crucial. If you find yourself saying things like "I feel like they don't like me" or "I feel like I'll never get that promotion," those are thoughts, not feelings. (In the back of this book in the Emotion Vocabulary section you will find a list of examples of feeling words so you can expand your emotion vocabulary.)

In this example, after exploring some options, we identify that this person is feeling afraid of rejection, self-doubt, ambivalence, uncertain, intimidated, and worried.

The next step is to wonder, "What am I thinking that is triggering these feelings and having me stop myself from applying for a promotion or even taking initiative in my current role?" Also, be curious about what beliefs or values might contribute to the thoughts.

In this example, some of the thoughts include: "They will never promote me so why bother," "I am not smart enough or educated enough to take on that higher role," "I will have to work so much harder than I do right now," "I will have to give up my work flexibility if I get promoted," "All the other people who have been promoted seem better than me," "I have never earned that amount of money before. My family won't approve."

With thoughts like these, it's no big surprise that this person is feeling fear, self-doubt, ambivalence, etc. It is also likely at the root of why they are stopping themselves from growing in their career.

| THOUGHTS | FEELINGS | ACTIONS | RESULTS |
|---|---|---|---|
| They will never promote me so why bother. | Afraid of rejection | Not applying for a promotion. | Stuck in the same dead-end role for years. |
| I am not smart enough or educated enough to take on that higher role. | Self-doubt | Not taking initiative in current job role. | |
| I will have to work so much harder than I do right now. | Ambivalence | | |
| I will have to give up my work flexibility if I get promoted. | Uncertain | | |
| All the other people who have been promoted seem better than me. | Intimidated | | |
| I have never earned that amount of money before. My family won't approve. | Worried | | |

Please remember the goal here isn't to be hard on yourself or beat yourself up because you are thinking or feeling like this and have been stopping yourself from growing. Don't do that. If you notice that you are having a lot of self-directed negative thoughts or internal name-calling, *stop* yourself immediately. Calling yourself stupid or dumb because you realize you are holding yourself back isn't helpful. Take a deep breath.

Remember, we're talking about evolving and this chapter is about self-discovery. You are learning about your way of thinking, feeling, and being so that you can choose to make changes if you want to. You won't identify what to change if you are too hard on yourself. Remember, curiosity. Be curious. Develop the awareness. Then wonder, "Ok, so this is where I am, how do I shift this?"

Because this book isn't about magical thinking, I am not going to tell you that all you would need to do, in this example, is change the way you think, and you will automatically get a promotion. But I can tell you that changing *how* you think and feel will have you changing your actions and behavior and *that*, ultimately, could lead you to a new role if that is what you actually wanted.

Here's what that might look like:

You could start from the beginning and wonder what thoughts would change those feelings. Or you could choose the results you really *want* to have and then reverse engineer RESULTS > ACTIONS > FEELINGS > THOUGHTS

| THOUGHTS | FEELINGS | ACTIONS | RESULTS |
|---|---|---|---|
| I have many of the skills needed to succeed in that next role. I can acquire new skills and demonstrate that I can do them. I have a lot to contribute as a leader. My family loves and accepts me as I am and having more money will not change who I am. | Nervous Excited by the possibility Inspired Confident Energized Curious Optimistic Resilient Empowered | Take on two new projects to demonstrate skills and leadership. Take more leader training classes to grow and develop. Seek opportunities to contribute to decision-making. Apply for the two new leader positions that are coming up. | Promoted to new role as a leader. |

Use this graphic and create this table whenever you are wondering why you always feel a certain way or why a particular result is what it is. It gives you so much information to understand the inner workings of your thoughts and feelings.

And to quote Maya Angelou, "When you know better, you do better." We can do better.

# GETTING TO THE CORE OF SELF-AWARENESS

*Self-awareness is the cornerstone of all other leadership capabilities.*

Exceptional leadership hinges on the depth of self-awareness and continuous self-discovery. Beyond mere introspection, it involves understanding complex facets of our motivations, biases, and vulnerabilities. True leadership is about transcending the self; it's about how we relate to, inspire, and influence others around us.

Armed with this awareness, leaders can distinguish their personal biases from objective realities, facilitating informed decisions. Their heightened understanding also gives rise to empathy, which fosters connections within their teams. In the fast-paced, ever-changing world of business, these self-aware leaders not only adapt but thrive, leveraging their strengths while being proactive about areas that need growth.

This introspective journey also has profound implications for authenticity. As leaders delve deeper into understanding themselves, they project an authenticity that breeds trust, prompting a deep sense of loyalty among their teams.

Self-awareness is one of the four dimensions of emotional intelligence (EI), which is our ability to recognize and understand emotions in ourselves and others—and use this awareness to manage our behavior and relationships. It's a concept developed by Daniel Goleman, back in 1995 in his book titled *Emotional Intelligence: Why It Can Matter More Than IQ.*[1] You've no doubt heard of how IQ (intelligence quotient) reflects our intellectual capacity, but in recent years EI has been identified as being more correlated than IQ when it comes to how well staff—and leaders—will excel at work. EI correlates highly with successful leaders.

High IQ without high EI is not a recipe for success because EI is vital for healthy relationships.

In the realm of leadership and personal growth, while intelligence opens doors, it's emotional intelligence—fueled by self-awareness—that ensures we navigate those doors effectively, building connections and driving success.

## WHAT HAPPENS IF YOU DON'T DEVELOP THIS SKILL?

The ripple effects of a leader's lack of self-awareness can be profound. For instance, biases and emotional triggers might skew their decision-making, causing them to rely more on personal feelings than objective facts. This could lead to decisions that don't align with the best interests of the organization. And, when actions don't mirror words, trust among team members may diminish. After all, employees need to see consistent and reliable behaviors to truly believe in their leaders. The fallout? Team members might opt to leave if they feel overlooked or lack trust in leadership.

Consider the case of Tom, a high-achieving manager known for his technical expertise in a leading tech company. Despite his skills, Tom was often perceived as unapproachable and dismissive. Unaware of how his behavior impacted his team, he frequently dismissed their creative ideas, preferring his own tried-and-tested methods. His team, initially enthusiastic and innovative, gradually became more and more disengaged. A promising project, once brimming with potential, started to falter due to lack of creative input and team collaboration. Tom's lack of self-awareness and inability to recognize his own shortcomings (and do something about them) stifled his team's growth and impacted the organization's innovation trajectory and reputation.

When a leader doesn't recognize their own room for improvement, they might shy away from feedback, inadvertently stifling their growth potential. This can trap them in a cycle of repetitive mistakes, hindering not only their personal evolution but also the progress of the entire organization.

And if there's a culture where feedback isn't valued, employees may hesitate to voice concerns or challenge existing norms. This can stagnate progress and dampen innovation. Additionally, such leaders might miss subtle cues in team dynamics or misunderstand the genuine concerns of their team members. Conflict resolution becomes a challenge if the leader doesn't grasp their role in disagreements, leading to escalated tensions or unresolved issues.

In essence, self-awareness isn't merely a personal trait; it's an organizational imperative. Even a leader with stellar technical skills can inadvertently create hurdles without it, depriving the team of a nurturing, progressive, and innovative environment. Also remember that once you develop an awareness it's only the starting point; the real impact comes from taking informed actions to rectify the issues you've recognized.

# BLIND SPOT TO WATCH OUT FOR: SELF-AWARENESS TO COMBAT SELF-SABOTAGE

Self-sabotage is a silent but powerful barrier to a leader's success. It is pervasive, hides in your blind spot, and can subtly undermine your decisions, diminish your confidence, and shift the focus away from your growth. It's the conflict that exists between your conscious goals, and your deeply held unconscious beliefs that may contradict those goals. By turning inward and understanding our behaviors and motives, we can confront and combat the roots of self-sabotage, paving the way for success.

Every one of us, to varying extents, grapples with self-sabotage. Throughout my career, I've seen leaders miss deadlines, unintentionally jeopardize promotions, miss out on business opportunities, gotten themselves fired, and even pushed themselves close to the brink of bankruptcy. Recognizing these behaviors as self-sabotage is pivotal. Only by pinpointing these harmful patterns can leaders begin the process of change, redirecting their path towards growth instead of inadvertently steering towards failure.

Self-sabotage often stems from skewed belief systems, ingrained in us from family influences or exposure to harmful environments. These beliefs cultivate fears of rejection, humiliation, failure, and even success, causing our self-esteem to plummet. Most of all, we just don't feel good enough. And if you believe you are not good enough, you will do everything you possibly can to prove that you are not worthy of success. While many reference this phenomenon as "limiting beliefs," I believe that term barely scratches the surface. For many, these beliefs morph into something far more dangerous—deeply rooted, toxic patterns that can be unconsciously self-destructive. What's more, recognizing it and stopping yourself can be quite a challenge.

Over the years, we have all seen many celebrities with their self-sabotage patterns on full display. When I see celebrities whose behaviors are self-destructive and their lives are sliding into a hole, I can almost see what's coming. They are very talented at their craft and yet they are miserable. They live their lives in a goldfish bowl and their lifestyle brings with it constant criticism. They're "too thin," "too fat," "too old," too… *something.* And they are only as popular as their last good song, movie, or TV show. Yet, because they earn so much money, it's assumed that they must be happy. *Many aren't.*

Their self-esteem and identity are wrapped up in what the media and the public think of them, so they don't have a clear sense of their value outside of the spotlight. And without a clear sense of who they are, they are often in a lot of emotional pain. For some, drugs and alcohol are used to self-medicate the numbness and pain they may experience. For others, they are hell-bent on self-destruction because of their toxic belief system. They don't believe they're worthy of their success or "good enough" for some reason. Sadly, there are so many who have paid the ultimate price with their lives.

So, why should you care about these celebs self-destructing? Because your story is more similar to theirs than you realize. Ask yourself, "In what ways is my identity and my self-esteem wrapped up in the work I do?" or "In what ways am I a people pleaser and care too deeply about what other people think of me, and how does that influence my behavior?" Most people have beliefs that have them sabotaging themselves. And while you are hopefully not sabotaging or soothing yourself with drugs and alcohol, there are many other ways you are slowly killing your spirit, your mind, and your body.

In my case, when I think back to my graduate school days, when I was on the brink of being struck from the doctoral program and grappling with deep depression, I sometimes wonder if I was unknowingly sabotaging my own success. One of my professors once shared something that has stuck with me: many doctoral candidates never finish, stalling at the last hurdle—either by not completing their dissertations or by dropping out. Many end up with the "ABD" (all but dissertation) label. This professor believed that, for many, underlying beliefs about money, success, and education got in the way. Perhaps they felt undeserving of the degree or uncomfortable surpassing their parents' achievements. I remember firmly telling myself, "I won't be one of them. I'm getting my degree." Each time I hit a roadblock, I'd remember that vow and it became a beacon, guiding me until I finally earned my doctorate.

Signs of self-sabotage can be subtle. Can you identify with any of the below?

- Not wanting to ask for help if you're stuck on a task, even though you know it would benefit you.
- Not meeting deadlines or avoiding completing tasks.
- Avoiding applying for promotions.
- Engaging in conflict at work or with people close to you when you feel uneasy.
- Setting goals that are so high they are likely unachievable.

- Or, sometimes, setting goals that are too low because you don't believe you can achieve more.
- Consistent negative self-talk, which could be about work or your personal relationships.
- Undermining any success you have by picking out flaws or anything that went wrong.
- Needing reassurance and approval from others, and not being able to trust yourself.

Is it self-sabotage that is hindering your success?

Perhaps you're hesitant to take risks due to fear of rejection, or you feel like an imposter, doubting the success you've achieved. Or maybe you're held back by paralyzing perfectionism, thinking mistakes are fatal errors and therefore always turn your work in late.

To combat these debilitating beliefs, it's essential to build new neural pathways. The first step is recognizing these negative thoughts, beliefs, and behavior patterns. Then reflect on their impact on your life and work. Remember, real change comes from actively adjusting your mindset. Things only change when you practice changing them—one thought, one belief at a time. Self-awareness gives you the keys to get started.

# HACKING YOUR SELF-AWARENESS

Alright, so you've started to pinpoint some of those limiting beliefs and thoughts that might be holding you back. Now what? Well, exploring self-awareness isn't necessarily about grand revelations overnight. It's more like piecing together a puzzle. Every piece represents a thought, a belief, or a behavior. And just like any puzzle, you start by examining each piece closely.

What's its shape? Its pattern? How does it fit with the others? Similarly, by examining and questioning your thoughts and beliefs, you gradually build a clearer picture of yourself. What are the patterns you are noticing and how do they fit? It's a journey, and it starts with curiously discerning the importance of each thought and belief, no matter how insignificant they might seem.

Here are some options to practice to get started:

# 1. Look at the big picture

During your reflections, taking a closer look at the complexities of your life story can be enlightening. Think about it: those memorable moments, the challenges you've overcome, and even the unexpected detours—they've all shaped you. The stories you've consistently told yourself play a big role in how you view the world. By unpacking these narratives, you're essentially doing reps for your self-awareness muscle. And like any good workout, it'll only get easier and more effective over time.

Here's an exercise I think will help:

Spend some quiet time gently reflecting on your life, how you were raised, the values and sayings that have shaped the way you think and what you believe, the people you've met along the way, the joys and even the difficult times you've experienced. Then, in a journal...

- Write down three things that have happened in your life that you believe might have shaped who you are.
- List three people who have made a positive difference to your life and why.
- Identify three specific moments that have stuck with you and what made them significant.
- Then list three sources of great happiness and three times you overcame a significant struggle.

The idea here is to get to know yourself better. Be curious and open to whatever comes up. Take a deep breath and see what naturally pops into your consciousness.

When you begin to understand yourself better, you learn what you may need to focus on to improve your life and work. The interesting thing about this task is that you're likely to think about or remember different aspects of your life each time you repeat it. It is really, really important that you don't become judgmental or critical of yourself. It takes great courage to go on this journey; do so with empathy and compassion.

## 2. Acknowledge patterns of thought and emotion

Self-awareness is the journey of tuning in and connecting with your inner thoughts and emotions.

Reflect on those moments when you've experienced a lack of engagement and a sense of disconnection at work. Not just distracted by other unrelated matters but putting in less effort than usual without really knowing why. With sharpened self-awareness, you can trace back to that exact moment a negative thought crept in, affecting your mood and, subsequently, your actions. Maybe it was offhand feedback or a curt email that made you think, "*I'm not cut out for this*" or "*They just don't like me.*"

Recognizing these emotional and thought patterns is something you refine over time. Here's a tip: flex that curious observer muscle.

Ask yourself the following questions:

- Why am I feeling like this?
- What made me react that way?
- Why did those words slip out?
- What's causing this emotion?
- What spurred that thought?

Tune in when you notice shifts in your mood—either a dip or a surge. Reflect on your actions, who you have spent time with, upcoming events, diet, or even what you might be missing at the moment. Ask yourself: What am I doing? What have I been doing? Who am I with? What do I have coming up? What have I eaten? What am I lacking right now?

Mindfulness meditation can be a real ally here. It helps to quiet the internal noise, grounding us firmly in the present. When those stray thoughts about work, dinner plans, or pending chores drift in, simply notice, acknowledge, and release them. But we'll look more closely at that in Chapter 7.

## 3. Consistently be curious

Curiosity pushes you to explore uncharted territories, build relationships, and seize opportunities. However, not everyone naturally possesses this trait. As people grow in their self-awareness, their innate curiosity tends to surface. And those who tap into it often find their relationships becoming healthier and more rewarding.

I often prompt my clients to dig deeper within themselves by considering questions like:

- How did I feel when X happened?
- Where in my body do these feelings arise?
- What challenged me today?
- Is this serving me well or holding me back?
- When did I first experience X?

Developing curiosity is an ongoing journey, take the time to keep practicing it.

## 4. How to discover your blind spots

To lead effectively, recognizing your blind spots is indispensable. These are the aspects of yourself that might be clear to others but remain hidden to you because they are just beyond what is obvious to you. And remember, blind spots aren't just your weaknesses or challenges; they might also be strengths you're unaware of.

Choose one or two people you have a strong relationship with—a family member, a close friend, and perhaps a trusted colleague so you can get comprehensive information. Their honesty will be invaluable, as you want someone who will give clear and direct feedback. Doing this exercise requires trust, so please keep that in mind as you consider the person you select to help you with this exercise.

Instead of a broad question like, "What are my weaknesses?" be more specific: "What have you noticed about my communication?" Or "How can I improve my communication in meetings?"

When this trusted person shares their perspective, listen. Don't get defensive or jump to explanations. Yes, hearing about blind spots can be uncomfortable, but it's vital feedback. Always express gratitude for their honesty, even if you need time to process what they've shared.

Don't think of this as a one-time exercise. Periodically check in with multiple individuals to gather a comprehensive understanding of your blind spots.

## SELF-MANAGEMENT: WHY IT MATTERS

While self-awareness is the compass that guides you along the path, self-management is how you actively steer yourself in the right direction. It's one thing to recognize your emotions, triggers, or behaviors, but another entirely to *actively* control and direct them in ways that benefit you, your team, and your organization.

*Think of it like this: self-management is managing the behavioral expression of your emotions, so they don't become out of control and cause conflict.*

A leader who excels in self-management exemplifies emotional intelligence. They use their self-awareness to recognize when they're at risk of reacting impulsively and have the self-discipline to pause, reflect, and respond in a manner that's appropriate and constructive. It's this ability that ensures conflicts are de-escalated instead of intensified, morale is boosted instead of eroded, and the organizational culture remains healthy. After all, leaders' behaviors set the tone for the entire organization. If they can't manage their own actions and reactions, how can they be expected to manage a team or company effectively?

Understanding and mastering self-management is imperative, not just for leadership but for personal and professional success. Rooted in emotional self-control, it's about maintaining balance in the face of external pressures. In the workplace, proficiency in self-management bolsters productivity. Emotional stability enhances focus, time management, and task efficiency.

Those leaders who've truly sharpened their self-management skills stand out, not because they're the loudest or most visible, but because they emanate a positive outlook and maintain a calm demeanor, even in turbulent situations.

Consider your own reactions during challenging times. How do you express your emotions? How do you behave when your stress levels rise? Reflecting on these questions will provide a clearer picture of your self-management skills. Be curious and assess yourself on a scale from 1 to 10. Where are you in regard to how well you're able to manage your emotional reactions and behavior?

Be honest on where you stand right now and continue to work on improving your skills. Cultivating them enhances not only personal well-being but also contributes to stronger, more genuine relationships.

- How do you express emotions under pressure?
- What's your default response when faced with stress?

- How well can you remain calm, especially in tense situations?
- Can you acknowledge mistakes readily?
- What issues or situations frequently trigger or derail you emotionally?
- How quickly does your anxiety or anger reach high intensity once triggered?
- How long does it take you to get calm again after an intense reaction?

Your answers provide insight into your self-management capabilities.

Being curious about how you express your emotions and manage your behavior during stressful times helps you see what your self-management skills are like.

# MANAGING YOUR EMOTIONAL REACTIONS AND BEHAVIOR

Once you begin being able to identify how you react in different situations, the key is to improve how you manage the expression of your emotions to reduce impulsivity and be able to respond appropriately.

## 1. Assess your body

A good exercise to cultivate both self-awareness and self-management is learning to notice what your body is doing. When you get nervous or angry, where do you first begin to feel it in your body? What signals does your body give you?

For example, notice your heartbeat: how fast is it beating? Your breathing: how fast or slow are you breathing? And how deeply? Do you tend to hold your breath when you concentrate or when you are speaking, or maybe when you are anxious or angry? What's your body temperature? Do you feel hot? Or cold? Do you notice any tension in your body? Does your chest feel tight? Your jaw? Do you clench your jaw or grind your teeth? What kinds of situations make your heart beat faster? What brings butterflies to your stomach? Do you clench your fists when you are getting annoyed or angry?

Over the years, I have learned exactly what my body does when I get nervous: my heart beats faster, my breathing gets faster and more shallow, and I feel really hot. I also notice that my mind feels like it is spinning. I know that all this happens because my adrenaline has spiked, and my fight or flight system has been activated. So, I also understand that the most important thing to do is calm myself down so I can regulate my heartbeat, breathing, and body temperature. I do a lot of things that make me nervous... and they are also exciting and fun. Speaking on stages and being on television are two things that trigger this nervous reaction in me, pretty much every single time! And yet I still do it. Why? Because I really enjoy doing it. I've noticed it's more the anticipation of the event than the event itself that brings about this intense anxious energy. When I am being interviewed or actually start speaking at an event, I'm fine.

At a recent speaking engagement, as I was sitting in my hotel room waiting for my time slot, I could feel the nervousness start to build in my body. And then I noticed (thanks to my Fitbit) that my heart rate (usually in the 60s–70s) was racing. Even though I was doing some deep breathing, it wouldn't fully slow down, because my mind kept wondering if everything was going to be ok. At one point, as I was putting on my makeup, I noticed that my heart rate had reached the 120s! It was like my body was going through a workout, but it was only because of nerves. I looked at myself in the mirror and said, "You really need to calm down, everything *is* fine, and it is going to *be* fine." I did some more deep breathing exercises to manage my breathing, spoke to a friend to distract myself, and had a long conversation with myself to settle the anxious thoughts going through my mind. "You can do this," I told myself. "You know what you're talking about. You've got this." This helped my mind settle, and my breathing and heart rate started slowing down. In the end, I left the room early to join the audience and experience their energy and enjoy the talks before mine. This was a great distraction for my mind and helped me maintain control over my mind and body.

In addition to what I have already mentioned, I also learned that shaking the nervous energy out of your body also works beautifully. It might look a bit weird to do in public, but I have been known to find a corner and shake my arms wildly around my body, shake each leg, and then wiggle my body. It shifts your energy and gets that tension outside of your body.

When these feelings come up in your body, don't try and prevent them, it is normal for your feelings to come up as an expression of what you are thinking or experiencing. Pay attention and notice what comes up first. And then what happens in your body. This way you will be able to recognize the patterns more quickly each time they show up and be able to stop them if needed.

If the emotion isn't helpful and you need a quick reset, always start with deep breathing because it can slow the heart rate, stabilize blood pressure, and lower stress reactions in the moment, so it's a brilliant skill to master.

## 2. Think before you act

Our internal dialogue holds immense power. The things you keep repeating in your mind become the lens through which you view the world. It impacts your personal relationships as well as your interpersonal connections at work. As I mentioned before, navigating your thought patterns and managing their impact can be challenging. Yet, truly understanding them can profoundly shift your reactions. Before you impulsively react, especially when emotions are high, tune into your inner dialogue. What are you whispering to yourself? How's it making you feel? Gift yourself a brief pause to digest it all before responding. It's like giving your mind a momentary break, a quick pit stop to determine the most appropriate response.

What is your self-talk telling you? Is it completely accurate or is it telling you a story that may not be true or correct? If you were to choose to respond with empathy, how would you respond? And what do you think the best response would be?

# 3. Focus on adaptability

Life, particularly in the workplace, is filled with unpredictability. It definitely keeps things interesting! While change can be unsettling, it's also an inevitable facet of our existence. Naturally, many of us are resistant to sudden shifts or alterations in the status quo that we weren't expecting, and that resistance can affect how we deal with it. However, embracing change, rather than avoiding it, is crucial.

Adaptability is a paramount quality for any leader. It's not just about adjusting to new scenarios but also about recognizing the potential in both the changing circumstances and the people involved. Embracing flexibility allows you to collaborate effectively with diverse teams and navigate the myriad of personalities that accompany them. When faced with change, the adaptable leader doesn't retreat; they assess the situation, anchor themselves in the present, and chart a course forward, ensuring stability even amidst fluctuation.

To improve your ability to adapt to different situations, it can be helpful to follow the following three steps:

1.  Learn from others who you admire who deal with tough situations well. Take mental notes when they are managing a tricky situation—how do they act, how do they speak, how do they manage others?
2.  Focus on the positives, or the silver lining, as some may say. It's not always easy, but when change comes around there is often a benefit to it. What is that benefit? What can you do/see/hear/watch now that you couldn't before?
3.  Be willing to make mistakes. It's not always easy, and you may have the best intentions, but trying to adapt—peacefully and calmly—at a time where you really don't feel peaceful and calm takes practice. And a lot of self-reflection. But the more aware you are at handling your thoughts and emotions, the

more likely your behaviors will naturally feel easier to manage at different moments in time.

# HOW THIS ALL LEADS TO INSIGHTS AND ACTION

*People need to know that they have all the tools within themselves. Self-awareness, which means awareness of their body, awareness of their mental space, awareness of their relationships—not only with each other, but with life and the ecosystem.*

DEEPAK CHOPRA

You have everything you need.

Improving your skills within emotional intelligence often comes down to unlearning what you've already learned (more on that later!). But the above opens up your world by stopping you living your life on autopilot.

The simple idea of being more aware really can lead to a more fulfilling life. It allows us to see things from the perspectives of others, work creatively and productively, and feel better about ourselves. Ultimately, studies show it leads to better decision-making.[2]

A study at Cornell University alongside Green Peak Partners in 2010 found that out of the 72 executives they analyzed, "a high self-awareness score was the strongest predictor of overall success." The researchers said: "The executives most likely to deliver good bottom line results are actually self-aware leaders who are especially good at working with individuals and in teams."[3]

When we're self-aware, we learn from our mistakes. We ask for feedback. We know what we need to improve. We can fully embrace who we are authentically, without the need to rely on others for validation. We put ourselves in the perfect position to learn new things, to be curious.

## APPLYING THE LEARNING

Based on what you've read in this chapter, ask yourself the following questions:

- What have you learned?
- What are your areas of growth?
- How will you apply your learnings from this chapter in your work?

And then go a little deeper. Please be very specific.

- What two or three things are you going to start doing? _____
- What two or three things are you going to stop doing? _____
- What two or three things do you already do that you can continue doing? _____

## Self-Reflection Questions

1. What are three core beliefs that drive my decisions and actions at work, and how do they align with my current professional path?

2. When faced with high-pressure situations, what strategies do I use to maintain composure and clarity, and how effective have they been in past situations?

3. How do I react to unexpected changes or disruptions in my work environment, and what strategies do I employ to adapt effectively?

## Exercises

Complete Exercises 1 and 2 (pp. 189–91).

If you need additional writing space, consider using a notebook to journal your thoughts.

# 2

# Rewriting the Script: The Unlearning Process of Self-Discovery and Growth

*You must unlearn what you have learned.*
YODA, *THE EMPIRE STRIKES BACK*

In the Star Wars movie, *The Empire Strikes Back* (1980), there is a central scene that unfolds on the murky planet of Dagobah where Luke Skywalker is with R2-D2, his loyal droid companion, and Yoda, the wise old Jedi Master. Luke is trying to raise his X-Wing Starfighter out of the swamp as it is submerging. As Luke struggles to raise the X-Wing, doubt plagues him. The problem is that Luke doesn't believe it's something that can be done. He doesn't believe *he* is capable of raising it because the X-Wing is such a heavy object and the only things he has been able to levitate previously are stones.

His self-limiting beliefs become a tangible barrier, and he refuses to believe *anyone* would be capable of levitating the X-Wing. Observing this struggle, Yoda demonstrates for Luke the power of belief and mindset. With a calm, composed gesture, Yoda effortlessly raises the X-Wing, placing it safely on dry land. The message is clear: our deeply ingrained beliefs and perceptions can limit our capabilities.

What Luke demonstrates so brilliantly in this example here is how what we strongly believe about ourselves and the world around us can prevent us from learning new things and persisting when things become challenging. The automatic cognitive scripts our brain has written and holds onto can interfere with our growth if we aren't paying attention. Yoda tells Luke that he must "unlearn what you have learned."

In essence, Yoda's wisdom serves as a timeless lesson for leaders and individuals alike. His advice to "unlearn what you have learned" is a reminder to question our automatic thoughts and behaviors, the scripts we often follow without thinking.

Expanding on the building a house theme mentioned in Chapter 1 where self-awareness was the solid foundation, this chapter will serve as the blueprint for your journey. Just as an architect re-evaluates and alters blueprints to construct a building that stands the test of time, this chapter will guide you in examining and restructuring your internal script. We'll discover how to redesign your mental architecture, clear away the obsolete structures of old beliefs and habits, and lay down new, robust frameworks that support your growth and leadership potential.

As we first explore how the brain functions, remember this: our brains aren't rigidly set in stone. They are flexible and can change, adapt, and even rewire themselves. This ability gives us the power to break free from limiting beliefs.

## HOW THE BRAIN FUNCTIONS

*Neurons that fire together, wire together.*

DONALD HEBB

I have always believed that if you understand how the brain works, how it's wired, and its primary purposes, you will better understand how and why people behave the way they do.

Our brains are fascinating, distinctive structures, influenced by both our genetics and our lived experiences. These individualized neural networks govern our cognitive abilities, emotional responses, and problem-solving skills, making each of us unique in how we are equipped to navigate the world. While these inherent pathways create certain predispositions, the brain's adaptability, governed by Hebbian learning (named after psychologist Donald Hebb[4]), allows us to rewire these networks. The brain's ability to do this is defined as "neuroplasticity."

This neuroplasticity enables neurons to forge new connections when activated simultaneously, which becomes more efficient with repeated activation. These dynamic neural pathways are the foundation for our thoughts, behaviors, and emotion regulation.

Put simply, neurons are activated when our brain learns something new, and then they connect with other neurons through synapses, forming a network. At first, the connections are weak, but they get stronger the more you repeat the action. So, with repeated practice of new habits, you create new neural networks and change your existing wiring—illustrated by the phrase, "Neurons that fire together, wire together." This is how you can train your brain to learn new thoughts and beliefs to shift your feelings and behavior.

Our brain also develops mental shortcuts based on our experiences and societal norms. These cognitive scripts are useful for efficient decision-making but can become outdated or counterproductive. As we saw with the Star Wars example of Luke Skywalker and the X-Wing, it can also prevent you from being open to expanding yourself to something beyond what is usual or comfortable for you. For leaders aiming for excellence, it's about learning new scripts and unlearning obsolete ones. This mental revision is essential for encouraging innovation and preventing biases from impacting our decision-making process.

The role of the brain extends far beyond learning and unlearning; it also operates to ensure our safety and make sense of our environment. Whether it's the adrenaline rush from high-stakes activities like riding motorcycles and skydiving, or the serenity that comes from gardening, hiking, or swimming, our unique preferences are a testament to the brain's complex architecture.

While everyone's brain decides differently what it perceives as dangerous activities, the interesting thing about the brain is that it isn't able to accurately assess the difference between real danger (a lion chasing you) and perceived danger (speaking on a stage in front of 200 people). In your brain and in your body, they feel similar. Your brain will tell you some version of "We are going to die if you do this!" and you have to fight the urge to flee or freeze.

Nestled deep in our brain, just in front of the hippocampus, is a small, almond-shaped structure called the amygdala. It is a part of the limbic system, which regulates emotion and encodes emotional memory. I call it the "fire alarm" of your brain because the amygdala is also primarily responsible for activating the fight-flight-freeze response when there is a dangerous threat. When it senses danger, it goes off.

The wonderful thing about this system being activated when there is an actual threat is that there's an immediate decision about whether fight-flight-or-freeze is the best response for survival and the body responds instantly to the situation. Adrenaline and cortisol are released into the bloodstream and the body readies itself to fight or flee if possible, and to freeze or hide when it's not. When this system is activated, the frontal lobe of the brain (the thinking and cognitive processing part of the brain) goes offline. You will often hear of people "acting without thinking" in a crisis— this is why. The brain has the body run on automatic pilot in order to survive the situation. Only once the immediate danger has passed does the frontal lobe come back online and begin to try and process what has just happened. Memories may be fragmented and distorted, and the brain creates a narrative from the experience (which may not be accurate).

Oftentimes, however, this system also gets activated in times of high stress when there is no actual threat of bodily harm. In these situations, there is a concern of failure, rejection, or humiliation that you experience in exactly the same way as if you were being chased by a lion. Your heartrate speeds up, blood pressure increases, breathing becomes shallow. You *feel* like you are in danger. In these situations, the frontal lobe (the thinking part of the brain) again goes offline.

The problem here, though, is that in *these* situations you *need* the thinking part of your brain to work. Imagine, you are about to take your driving test, licensing exam, or bar exam, go in for an important interview for your dream job, walk out onto a stage to speak to an audience, or give a presentation at an important meeting, and your mind goes completely blank. I've heard it so many times, "My mind went blank, and I couldn't remember anything!" Not exactly an opportune time for your brain to go missing, is it? Unfortunately, when this happens and people don't know how to handle it, their anxiety increases and the story that gets created by their own mind is that they are incapable. Which isn't true.

So, what can you do to get your brain back and functioning the way you need it to? Honestly, it is so simple, you probably aren't going to believe me... but it is truly the most important skill you can use to regulate how your emotions impact your mind and body.

Breathe.

Yes, breathe. Take a deep inhale breath, exhale, and then take another. Continue slowly and deeply inhaling and exhaling until your heart rate feels like it is getting back to normal. Once your heart slows down, so will everything else and you will notice your fight/flight responses slowing and your body regulating back to normal. Then your frontal lobe will come back online. The great thing is that this doesn't have to take a long time. I always tell my clients and my friends, before you go into that meeting or take that test, *breathe*. Get centered for a moment and then take a deep breath and imagine yourself being successful.

Taking deeper breaths regularly is essential to managing your emotions and behavior more effectively. I have taught everyone from young children to older adults exactly how this one tool can change everything. I have used it to support raging teens in a psychiatric hospital to feel in control of their body and emotions and manage their behavior without staff intervention, and help a young woman slow down a panic attack she was having in my office.

You can't *tell* someone to calm down in an intense situation or reason with them when their amygdala has hijacked their cognitive functioning. But supporting them to breathe and get back in control of their body and mind helps them get into a more controlled mental state to think more clearly.

# DO YOU KNOW WHAT YOU BELIEVE—AND WHY YOU BELIEVE IT?

From the moment we're born until the present day, our brain is taking in information through our senses from the world around us. As it takes in that information, the brain processes and filters it, and then decides what meaning to give it and where to file it.

As we grow up, our parents, family members, peers, teachers, religious figures, the media, and social media contribute to how we think and what we believe. What they say and do shapes how we think about gender, race and ethnicity, wealth, work, what it means to be intelligent or educated, and what we believe is possible for us to achieve.

But oftentimes, what we believe isn't helpful or true. Well-meaning people give us inaccurate information. Not to mention that any challenging or traumatic experiences you have can completely distort how your brain views the world and your place in it.

## The reality of unconscious biases

Many people resist the idea that they have unconscious biases. I think it's because they believe it is something to feel shame about and there is stigma attached to it. When people are afraid of being judged, they try to hide what is right in front of them. The truth is that we all have biases. You, me, all of us.

This is a simple fact of human psychology. If you have a brain, you have biases. Our brains are wired to make quick judgments and assessments of our surroundings, which is a necessary function for survival and decision-making. Unfortunately, this process is not infallible.

Our brain loves to fill in knowledge gaps with assumptions based on past experiences, which, while efficient, are not always accurate. These automatic, deeply ingrained assumptions are what we refer to as unconscious biases. They influence our decisions and actions, often without our awareness.

Understanding this is the first critical step towards addressing and mitigating their impact on our behavior and decisions.

As a leader or hiring manager, can you see why this is important?

If you are not conscious of your biases, they may be impacting your hiring and promoting decisions. They may cause you to listen to the ideas of some people more closely in meetings than others. For example, if you have a belief that millennials are entitled and aren't interested in putting real effort into their work, you may overlook a great employee simply because you have a bias towards their generation that may be completely inaccurate.

When you are willing to be curious about your biases and develop self-awareness about them, you can see how your thoughts are shaped by "unconscious" forces—and what influence this then has on how you feel or act. But just being aware that you have biases isn't enough. It is important to take action to unlearn them.

I teach my clients how their brain's conditioning has led to their current beliefs, behavior patterns, and biases, and how to work on their brain intentionally to cultivate new thoughts that will move them towards different results. Once we become aware of our beliefs and biases and own them— we have the power to change them.

## Why does this matter if you are a leader?

Leadership is not only about possessing a wealth of information but also about demonstrating the adaptability and openness to challenge preexisting notions. Markets evolve, employee needs change, and what worked yesterday may not be the solution for tomorrow. A leader's ability to unlearn old habits and patterns makes room for innovative thinking and problem-solving.

Importantly, this includes unlearning ingrained biases, outdated beliefs, and obsolete values that can skew interpersonal relationships and create disparities in hiring and promotions within a team. When leaders champion the principle of unlearning, they set a standard for the entire team, cultivating a culture where employees feel encouraged to question their assumptions, learn, and thrive.

At various stages in my own life, I've had to critically examine the foundational assumptions that were guiding my actions and confront the misguided beliefs and self-doubts that were circulating through my mind. It took time for me to unlearn these unhelpful thought patterns and forge new neural connections so that I could grow both personally and professionally.

One very significant time was towards the end of my doctoral training journey when I found myself on the verge of expulsion. Battling severe depression and feeling abandoned by the people who were meant to mentor and guide me, I persevered and remained in the program through a loophole. The emotional residue of that experience of being able to stay due to a technicality clung to me like glue for many years, shaping my self-perception as a professional and eroding my confidence in my abilities. It didn't matter that I had completed all of my classes with high marks and graduated as a student in "good standing" with a GPA of 3.86 (out of 4, for those unfamiliar with the US point system).

I questioned my worthiness to serve as a psychologist, let alone a leader, because of those struggles. In a profession where expertise and credibility are paramount, such self-doubt had significant implications. I spent the early years of my career as a psychologist trying to prove to myself (mostly) and to others that I belonged in this career, and that I had the right to help others. Every new potential elevation in my career had me wondering, "What if I am not really cut out for this?"

And then I finally started to understand that I had control over what my mind spent time ruminating on and that these beliefs I had were not serving me and were exhausting! This realization crystallized my commitment to unlearn these debilitating assumptions. I used to view my mind as an unchangeable constant, subjecting me to a predetermined narrative. But using the power of curiosity, and developing the self-awareness to identify the thoughts and beliefs that were obstacles keeping me stuck, enabled me to consciously untangle these limitations holding me back.

My personal growth transformation has been a long-term (and unfinished) adventure. Since venturing into self-employment 14 years ago, the evolution has been even more profound. To be an effective business owner and leader—of both myself and others—I have come to understand that growth is not optional but essential. We must continue to evolve so we can expand and elevate into new levels of success.

Leadership, much like personal growth, is not a static endeavor but a perpetual cycle of adaptation and innovation. Just as individuals wrestle with mental narratives that challenge their worth, leaders face periods of doubt and uncertainty. The key to navigating this complex landscape is mental agility, which serves as a form of "leadership fitness." This continuous effort not only helps dismantle old paradigms but also fosters the adoption of new perspectives. Through this consistent introspection and reframing, leaders not only forge new neural pathways for themselves but also contribute to building more adaptive and healthier organizations.

## UNLEARNING THE OBSTACLE OF SELF-SABOTAGE

We know leaders—like many others—will face periods of doubt at various stages in their lives and careers. And that doubt can cause self-sabotage. In Chapter 1, we identified that the first step of the journey is becoming aware of this "undermining" you may be subconsciously doing to slow down or stop your progress.

Once you are aware, you now must acknowledge it, recognize it, and learn that it can be changed if you want to change it.

It reminds me of a friend of mine with dyslexia who, now in his 50s, told me that as a child he thought he was "dumb" because at school his teachers didn't know how to support students with dyslexia. These students were treated as though they didn't have the ability to learn. He didn't do particularly well in school and spent the better part of his life fighting against an internal voice telling him he was stupid. It impacted what he believed he could achieve and meant that he often assumed people didn't want to hear what he had to say. He realized how important it was for him to release the emotion and unlearn the belief that had him continuously repeating that he wasn't capable.

When people stick to the same patterns of thinking, they'll keep running into the same obstacles and getting the same results. To break free, you must rewrite your mental scripts. Understanding the "why" behind your blocks is the first step in dismantling them. One often overlooked factor in this process is kindness—especially when grappling with negative self-talk or self-destructive behaviors. When working to overcome these ingrained patterns, it's crucial to extend compassion towards yourself, especially when faced with setbacks or when catching yourself in negative self-talk.

Self-sabotage is rooted in long-standing habits that become your go-to coping mechanisms. When you hit familiar obstacles—doubting your worth or hesitating to seek that promotion, for instance—you can now recognize them for what they are: barriers to growth. Once you do that internal growth work, the next time you hit the obstacle again, you'll recognize it and be able to move forward more quickly. But that doesn't mean the obstacle will never be there—it means it's much quicker to move past.

## PRACTICING MINDFULNESS

It's helpful to learn to sit with these feelings of low self-worth, and practice being gentle with yourself as they come up. Focusing on your breath and allowing your thoughts to come and go can strengthen your ability to stay present in the moment (which you'll need when that inner critic crops up). This is mindfulness. It involves cultivating an awareness of your thoughts, emotions, and bodily sensations, so you can better take notice of damaging thoughts as they come up.

There are so many ways to practice mindfulness, but try this simple, three-minute activity first.

- Sit comfortably, with your feet touching the floor.
- Drop your shoulders, relax any tense muscles, and take in three long, slow and deep breaths. Don't worry too much about counting at this stage. Those three breaths will bring you into the moment, then you can relax into your normal breathing pattern.
- Now scan down your body, bit by bit, and relax every single part you come across: your forehead, your eyebrows, your eyelids, your nose, your mouth, down to your neck and your shoulders. Relax your arms, your chest, your stomach. Keep scanning down your body, relaxing.
- If thoughts enter your mind during this exercise, acknowledge them, then let them pass. You might find it useful to set a timer on your phone for this and stay in the moment until it goes off.

How do you feel once you open your eyes?

# EXPLORING PRACTICAL STRATEGIES FOR UNLEARNING

Unlearning is not about erasing or discarding our preexisting knowledge; it's more about acquiring the wisdom to entertain alternative perspectives and make more intentional choices. It's the mental agility that allows us to recognize when an existing belief or mindset no longer serves us and have the courage to change direction. And while unlearning may touch on a myriad of ingrained habits and biases, it's a marathon, not a sprint—a lifelong journey to enhance your leadership expertise and overall well-being.

## Embrace the journey

*It's a marathon, not a sprint.*

Being curious about your mental conditioning isn't a one-time event but an ongoing process. While it's possible to pick up new skills quickly, they often need fine-tuning as you grow. The journey includes trial and error, self-reflection, and the occasional setback.

Life (and work) will always throw curveballs your way, and your responsibility is to adapt and grow through these challenges. It requires the continuous ability to question and reassess your thoughts and actions.

A former client—we'll call her Alex—was a well-respected manager at her company, but she was reluctant to apply for a newly posted executive position. Despite a successful track record, Alex carried an ingrained belief from childhood that she was "just not leadership material." In an exchange with a teacher during middle school, she was told, "You'll never amount to anything." Although she was well qualified and highly skilled, this kept twirling around in the back of her mind like a mantra. This belief often had Alex feeling invisible in group settings and she was often expecting her senior leaders to realize she was a "fraud." She said she often felt like an imposter.

Our work together focused on learning where these beliefs came from, deciding they were unhelpful to her, and then creating new ones that gave her the confidence to use her voice in meetings and lead her team effectively. Alex couldn't remember much about the conversation with the teacher, but the statement "You'll never amount to anything" left an indelible imprint on her young mind. By realizing this one phrase was not her identity and had no power in her life unless she gave it power, she was able to dismantle it. She identified and embraced her successes and started looking forward to achieving new ones.

Several months later, Alex applied for a director role and got it. The self-doubt didn't magically disappear; she must still catch herself from falling into old thought patterns. However, she has cultivated the awareness to identify these moments and the skills to navigate them more effectively.

## Pay attention to the language you're using in your self-talk

It's not crazy to talk to yourself.

We all engage in self-talk. It's the inner dialogue we have that shapes our perception of ourselves and the world around us. But how often do we pause to consider the language we're using in this private conversation? The words and phrases you choose in these moments don't just reflect your thoughts; they can also shape your behavior, influence your interactions, and ultimately dictate your success or failure.

Recognizing self-sabotage starts with tuning into what you're telling yourself. Writing down the statements you say to yourself like "I can't do that," "I won't be able to get that promotion," or "I'm not good enough," puts in plain view how these thoughts can undermine your well-being and hold you back.

Your inner critic isn't just a nagging voice; it's a mental construct that represents your doubts, fears, and insecurities.

Often, this critic is a product of past experiences, societal expectations, or even early life teachings that have been internalized over time. While its intention might originally have been protective—to keep you from venturing too far out of your comfort zone—it can become a hindrance in your professional and personal growth. Recognizing that this voice is not an objective truth but rather a skewed perspective allows you to challenge its claims and replace them with more empowering beliefs.

I playfully named mine "Critical Christina" or sometimes "Negative Nelly," depending on what they are saying at any given moment. And when they get too noisy or are disrupting my thoughts and mood, I make a note of what they are saying and then ask them nicely to please be quiet and give them something to cheer me on about. It's quite effective!

So, what name will you give your inner critic? Some of my clients have named theirs Negative Nick and Critical Chris. Some have gotten even more creative and named them after known villains like "Volde" (short for Voldemort from *Harry Potter*) or Darth Vader from the Star Wars movies. Feel free to get creative and pick something memorable to help yourself separate that critical voice from the rest of your thoughts when necessary.

And what's your self-talk focused on? If it's primarily about limitations, flip the script. Instead of focusing on what could go wrong, what you can't do, start focusing on the gifts you have, the strengths you hold, and what would go right. Make it a daily habit to ask: what is my inner voice saying? Am I being self-critical?

## Embrace the discomfort of change

Humans don't like change, and yet change is said to be the one constant in life.

Change is inherently uncomfortable, largely because it disrupts our familiar patterns and habits. The "unknown" can seem scary and can bring up feelings of anxiety and nervousness. However, unlearning requires embracing this discomfort as a necessary part of growth. Initially, the unease may be unsettling, but it's the gateway to new opportunities and a better version of yourself.

Start by acknowledging your discomfort. A simple internal statement like, "I'm feeling uncomfortable because this is new to me," sets the stage for a more constructive approach.

Then shift your focus to the benefits of the change you're considering. Identify at least three positive outcomes that could arise from adopting a new mindset or behavior.

It's often helpful to share your journey with a trusted individual. Expressing your feelings and intentions can not only lighten your emotional load but also offer valuable outside perspective.

Lastly, remember that growth happens outside your comfort zone. Rather than retreating at the first sign of difficulty, navigate through it. Utilize techniques like mindfulness or deep breathing exercises to manage your discomfort and continue moving forward.

## Prioritize what's important

Much of our daily lives revolve around routines and habits. From the moment we wake up to when we finish working, many of our actions are performed almost on autopilot. But how many of these habits genuinely contribute to your sense of fulfillment or your long-term goals?

Prioritizing is more than just creating a to-do list; it's an act of conscious decision-making that assists you with identifying what truly matters to you. It is a transformative practice that can uncover your underlying values, aspirations, and even limitations. It gives you a lens through which to view your daily choices, pushing you to question and possibly unlearn ingrained habits that don't serve you.

Start by listing your day-to-day activities, especially in areas where you feel change is needed—be it your workday or your morning routine. Next, write down what genuinely matters to you and your goals. Compare these lists, and you'll likely find gaps between what you do and what you want to do. Use this as an opportunity to realign your actions with your objectives.

But don't just stop at list-making. Begin to make these prioritized actions a part of your day. It may feel uncomfortable initially, but remember, every small, conscious choice you make is a step towards personal and professional growth. Over time, these small new changes pave the way for more significant transformation, enriching your leadership journey and personal life. Prioritizing is not just about doing things right; it's about doing the right things, continually evolving, and growing in the process.

## Learn more by focusing on the new

Cultivate a habit of seeking out the new—be it ideas, strategies, or perspectives. The unfamiliar can be a catalyst for change and growth. Ask yourself regularly: "What don't I know yet? What more could I discover?"

Incorporate this principle into your daily routine. Take a different path during your walk, engage with a colleague you haven't spoken to, or consider fresh research for your next meeting. New information, new ideas, new people, new perspectives, new strategies. The idea is to step out of your comfort zone just enough to shake up your usual way of thinking. You'll not only broaden your horizons but could also stumble upon a transformative insight.

## Unlearn by learning from others

By this point, as you have grown attuned to your own cognitive patterns and the habits you aim to change, consider expanding your lens to be curious about others. How do they deal with situations? How do they start their day? How do they prioritize a long task list? How do they cope under stress? How is their behavior different from your own?

Observation can be a powerful tool—take notice of how people interact during meetings or behave on typical workdays. Alternatively, ask them directly. Reach out to those whose approach you admire and inquire about their methods. Doing so can offer insights that help refine your own practices and might lead to more successful results.

Conclude your self-discovery journey by incorporating lessons from trusted and admired colleagues. Their strategies might hold the key to unlocking your own next level of productivity and well-being.

# APPLYING THE LEARNING

Based on what you've read in this chapter, ask yourself the following questions:

- What have you learned?
- What are your areas of growth?
- How will you apply your learnings from this chapter?

And then go a little deeper. Please be very specific.

- What two or three things are you going to start doing? _____
- What two or three things are you going to stop doing? _____
- What two or three things do you already do that you can continue doing? _____

## Self-Reflection Questions

1. How do my existing values and beliefs, formed from past experiences and learnings, influence my current decision-making and behavior at work?
2. What specific values or beliefs might be limiting my growth or effectiveness?
3. How can I actively work to rewrite these scripts to better align with my current goals and the evolving needs of my team and organization?
4. What biases have I (or someone else) noticed in my decision-making processes and what steps can I take to address and mitigate them?

## Exercises

Complete Exercises 3–5 (pp. 191–3).

# 3

# Stay the Course: The Power of Commitment and Consistency

*Change only happens when you decide and commit.*

Having spent Chapter 1 on the transformative journey of self-discovery through self-awareness and self-management, we laid the groundwork for introspection. Understanding who you are and managing your behaviors and emotions are integral first steps, but they only set the stage. Chapter 2 then guided you through the essential process of "rewriting the script," helping you liberate yourself from outdated beliefs, unproductive habits, and restrictive mindsets that can inhibit growth. Yet, knowing yourself and shedding the old skin aren't enough to realize your full potential, either as a leader or as an individual. This is where Chapter 3 comes in.

As mentioned previously, think of the progression through these chapters as constructing a building. Self-awareness and self-management form the core and foundation, giving you a solid base to build upon. Rewriting the script serves as the architectural plan, the blueprint for constructing things in a new, more effective way. Now, commitment and consistency act as the materials and the labor. Without them, even the most thoughtful design and solid foundation cannot become a functional, thriving structure. It's your continued commitment to the blueprint and the consistent effort to build that turns vision into reality. Without staying the course, the transformation and growth made possible by self-awareness and a renewed personal script will likely remain unfinished projects. Therefore, mastering the art of commitment and consistency is crucial for ensuring that the foundational work you've done results in meaningful, long-lasting change.

In the workplace, commitment is the dedication and responsibility an individual shows towards their role, goals, and the organization's values. It reflects their willingness to persist in their efforts, align with team objectives, and contribute positively to the company's culture. Many people do *profess* a commitment to their goals, to personal growth, and to their teams. Yet, a large gap often exists between their words and action. Without commitment, even the most exciting plans falter, deadlines become fluid, and the ripples of inconsistency impact not just the leader and team, but also the entire organization.

Consistency, on the other hand, isn't merely about showing up; it's about showing up in a way that's aligned with your values, objectives, and responsibilities. It's what builds trust among team members and enables a culture of accountability and psychological safety. Consistency in leadership sends a powerful message: "I am committed to our collective success, to our well-being, and to an environment where each of us can thrive."

The harsh reality is that inconsistency is often the only consistent thing people do. It is definitely a challenge to remain consistent from day to day. Being inconsistent is a tendency that not only undermines your own growth but can also jeopardize the integrity of the team and the goals of the organization. This is why it becomes imperative for leaders to be unwavering in their commitments—to themselves, their teams, and the larger purpose they serve. The act of making a commitment is far less significant than the daily labor of keeping that commitment.

So, how do you bridge the chasm between intention and execution? How can leaders embody the consistency that nourishes a healthy, productive work environment? This chapter aims to delve into these essential questions, offering actionable insights to fortify your commitments and establish a lasting consistency that enriches both personal and professional landscapes.

# CREATING CHANGE FOR YOURSELF

Contrary to popular belief, creating meaningful change in your life doesn't have to be a monumental task. It can be quite simple. In fact, the secret lies in the subtleties—the incremental steps and seemingly minor decisions that accumulate over time. However, to initiate and sustain this change, two key ingredients are non-negotiable: unwavering commitment to your goals and consistent action to achieve them.

Commitment can be defined as being dedicated to an activity or behavior that you set out to do, until completion. It is the choice you make in the present that obligates you to a future outcome. Consistency is about the quality of behaving in the same way—or taking the same actions, for example—over a period of time. It's repeated practice. Showing by your repeated actions that you will do what you said you would do. The key thing here is that you need both. These two qualities are deeply interconnected; possessing both commitment and consistency effectively attaches you to the behaviors and outcomes you desire for the future.

Consider commitment your hidden superpower. Embarking on any new venture—personal or professional—will inevitably present obstacles and setbacks that could derail your progress. Commitment ensures you stay the course, providing you with the resilience needed to overcome challenges. Consistency, in turn, fortifies that commitment. It allows you to incrementally refine your skills or behaviors, creating a loop of continuous improvement. As the new adage goes, "Practice makes progress," but it's the commitment to practice consistently that truly makes the difference.

This is all well and good, but how do we commit to commitment? And how do we stay consistent with consistency?

## Accountability

*Accountability is the glue that ties commitment to the result.*
BOB PROCTOR

Accountability is worth mentioning here because it really is the glue that ties the commitments you make to the results you see. When you aren't fully committed and aren't holding yourself accountable to what you said you would do, the result you see will reflect that. You, by default, will likely end up not achieving what you set out to do.

Accountability means taking full responsibility for what you do and the results you are aiming for. It's an essential part of being committed and staying consistent. It's about being answerable for decisions, actions, and the outcomes—and it involves taking ownership for specific results. When you're accountable, you own your actions and their outcomes.

When it comes to personal accountability, it's all about making a plan for your future and then sticking to it. You take full responsibility for your own actions and outcomes, recognizing that *you* are the one who must stay the course and reach the finish line. This helps you reach your goals, boosts your self-confidence, and can result in a higher level of happiness. Sure, it takes extra effort, but the payoff is big. Staying committed to your goals requires strong willpower, but the rewards make it worth the effort.

Personal accountability is powerful. It is one thing to set a goal and say you are going to do it, but to actually stay committed and follow through with your goals is life changing.

An example of my own that I have shared with my clients—of when I truly committed to something and held myself personally accountable for the outcome—was back in August 2020. At the time, I thought that my commitment muscle was a little weak, and I wanted to see what would happen if I committed to doing something knowing there would be times when I didn't want to do it—would I do it even when I didn't feel motivated to do it?

I decided that I was going to walk five miles every day for three months. Every single day. No matter what. No matter if I was tired. If it was cold. If it was raining (as it so often does here in England). No matter how busy I was. No matter what. No matter what was going on, whether I felt like it or not, I committed to this five-mile walk.

And, I did it.

In the end, I actually walked five miles every day for ten months! I did it in the rain, in the sunshine, in the snow, in the hail, when it was cold, when I was sleepy, when I didn't feel up to it. I tested the strength of my commitment and consistency muscles, and it felt amazing to do exactly what I said I would do. One weekend during the initial three months, I walked 26 miles with a friend in one day—from Richmond to Walton-on-Thames and back—for the London virtual marathon. It was awful weather, but we did it. The next day, people assumed I would not bother with my daily five miles (after all, I'd done plenty more than that the day before), but I refused not to honor the commitment I had made. No excuses. I had to continue the commitment, and so I did. After ten months, I decided that I didn't want to walk this far every day anymore and changed my commitment.

Now, my goal is to go to the gym three times a week. My teenage daughter is also now setting small goals for herself. She recently set herself the goal of being able to run for one hour after starting from not running at all! She is building up her strength and stamina, but she is showing herself, and me, that when you make a commitment and accept no excuses, you keep going. As soon as we allow ourselves to make excuses, we stop. It is really great seeing her realize these important principles at such a young age. They will serve her well both now and in the future.

So... if you're looking for that great success, let me ask you one question: how strong is your commitment muscle?

## Your commitment muscle

Do you always follow through on what you set out to do? Or do you often cave in and give up? Are you one of those people who sets New Year's resolutions, secretly knowing that by March, your goal will probably have gone out the window already? Or do you only set realistic, achievable resolutions that you always carry through for the entire year? There is no judgment here, but it is important for you to be honest with yourself and have a clear starting point.

But if you are a part of the population who gives up by March, you aren't alone! Research from the University of Scranton indicates that a staggering 92% of people fail to achieve the goals they set at the beginning of the year.[5] In fact, most have lost their focus and commitment within a few months. Why? Probably because their commitment muscle was weak, and they made a "small c" commitment rather than a "Big C" commitment. The way I describe it to my clients, a Big C commitment is the "no excuses," no matter what commitment. When you make a Big C commitment, you don't give up on your goal. You persevere until completion. It is an unbreakable pledge you make to yourself.

So, what factors contribute to a weak commitment muscle? For one, our lives are inundated with various "should-dos" and "must-dos," leading to a feeling of inadequacy when we can't accomplish it all. We say "yes" to too many things and this feeling of falling short fuels a culture of comparison, undermining our commitment and causing us to question our capabilities.

Your inner critic is another major factor that affects the strength of your commitment muscle. We've previously discussed the necessity of unlearning the self-critical thoughts that we often fuel our mind with so we can prevent self-sabotage. Doubt can be your downfall, making you reluctant to commit because you don't believe you can achieve your goal. This self-imposed limitation hampers your progress in both your professional and personal spheres.

Prior failures can also inhibit future commitments. If you've set goals and failed to meet them before, it's understandable that you might hesitate to take on new challenges. However, it's crucial to recognize that setbacks are not predictive of future outcomes. By silencing your inner critic, you create a better atmosphere for commitment and, ultimately, success.

The good news is that your commitment muscle is not set in stone; it can be strengthened. Personally, I saw significant improvement when I committed to walking five miles daily. The secret lies in understanding that small, consistent actions lead to significant, worthwhile results.

The key to cultivating your commitment muscle is proving to yourself how making a single real Big C commitment to one achievable but challenging thing can bring worthwhile results.

# STOP WAITING TO FEEL MOTIVATED

I'm going to be blunt: motivation is a luxury most of us don't have time to wait for.

Relying on motivation is a risky strategy. Your to-do list doesn't pause when your motivation wanes. Whether the task at hand is wrapping up a report, delivering a presentation, or devising a strategy, it needs to get done. Motivation is a bonus, not a necessity. Commitment is the true driver that helps you reach your goals.

Once you've committed to something, the question of "feeling like doing it" should become irrelevant. Commitment means aligning your actions with your word, regardless of your emotional state. It's about integrity, not mood.

It's normal to struggle with motivation; what counts is honoring your commitments. Instead of pondering your motivation levels, redirect your focus to the commitments you're set to fulfill that day.

When I was walking for 10 months, especially the first three months, there were plenty of days I felt unmotivated.

It is super easy to feel that way when it is raining or dreary or hailing! The only thing that got me out the door was knowing that I couldn't break the pledge I had made to myself.

When roadblocks appear, it's easy to revert to old habits or neglect our commitments. The point is not to let fluctuating motivation levels derail you from what really matters. Your commitment muscle, especially when resolute, can override any lack of motivation you may experience.

Recent studies have shown motivation is a significant issue for many, even before the pandemic of 2020 disrupted work environments.[6] But the focus on motivation can be misleading. It's commitment that consistently delivers results, not the fluctuating state of being motivated.

Ask yourself regularly, "How committed am I to achieving my results? Am I willing to be consistent and remember this choice I made that obligates me to take regular action until I complete this task or goal?"

## Building trust through commitment and consistency

Trust is the secure base that holds any team or organization together, and its importance can't be overstated. In the context of the workplace, lacking trust can lead to a cascade of issues, ranging from team disengagement to reduced productivity. On the flip side, a high level of trust is associated with increased innovation, lower stress levels, and the enhanced overall well-being of employees. Commitment, consistency, and accountability are three important principles that contribute to building trust in an organization.

Consistency in actions and decision-making doesn't just make life easier for employees; it creates an environment where people feel safe and valued. In a stable and predictable setting, employees gain the confidence to act independently and make decisions without the constant fear of reprimand or conflict. When someone trusts you, they're more likely to want to work with you, help you, support you, collaborate with you, and champion you.

When a leader commits to something and follows through, it sets an example for the entire team and strengthens your credibility as a leader. There is nothing worse for your team than constantly being pulled in different directions. Whether it's meeting deadlines or delivering on project goals, consistent performance establishes a track record of reliability. This helps employees know that their leadership is committed and can be counted on—a key ingredient in the recipe for trust.

Consistency shouldn't stop at tasks and responsibilities; it also extends to emotional conduct. So, please do consider how you are showing up emotionally. Are you calm, present, and consistent? Or does your mood change with the wind and employees aren't sure how they'll be treated from day to day because it will depend on your mood? Leaders who manage their emotions well, especially during challenging times, offer a sense of stability and psychological safety. This emotional balance can be incredibly reassuring to employees, who look to their leaders as a compass in turbulent times.

When employees see that leadership values commitment and consistency because they are walking the talk and modeling this behavior at work, it incentivizes them to incorporate these qualities into their own work. Consistency then becomes a cycle, perpetuating a culture where trust is not only established but continually nurtured.

As humans, we have more trust in people who are clear with their intentions and consistent in their approach. Naturally, they seem more reliable because we know who they are and what they're about. They don't change their minds or behaviors often, resulting in irrational behaviors.

Yvon Chouinard, the founder of Patagonia, serves as an excellent example of how commitment and consistency can build trust and brand value. His unwavering dedication to environmental consciousness has set the standard, not just recently but for decades. As early as 1985, he committed to donating 1% of all sales to environmental causes through the

1% For the Planet initiative.[7] This long-term commitment has not just been about pledging profits; it's also about standing up for what he believes in.

Whether it's legal action against federal plans to reduce national monuments or relocating events to environmentally friendly states, Chouinard isn't afraid to make bold moves. Moreover, the company reinforces its core values through practical measures like their Tools for Activists conference, a shift to organic cotton in the 1990s, and transparent manufacturing processes.[8]

All these actions collectively contribute to a robust foundation of trust, both in Chouinard as a leader and in Patagonia as a brand. This long-standing consistency in commitment underscores why people feel good purchasing from Patagonia and how the brand has achieved remarkable success. In essence, Chouinard's leadership at Patagonia clearly demonstrates the business and ethical dividends that come from a genuine, consistent commitment to core values.

> *Commitment is what gets you started. Consistency is what gets you somewhere.*
>
> OMAR ITANI

# WAYS TO IMPROVE COMMITMENT AND CONSISTENCY

## Create SMART goals

Your personal commitment and consistency are amplified when they align with well-structured goals. Goals aren't just a list of aspirations; they're essential to any organization, serving as clear signals of what's important. They offer both inspiration and act as a guide. Furthermore, when these goals resonate with your team and align with the organization's mission, the impact can be extraordinary. So, it's not merely about setting goals; it's about setting the right kind of goals—SMART goals.[9]

These goals, an acronym for Specific, Measurable, Achievable, Relevant, and Time-Bound, allow you to crystallize your commitments into actionable steps. Developed originally by George Doran, Arthur Miller, and James Cunningham in 1981, this approach has long been recognized for its effectiveness in the workplace.

By setting SMART goals, you're not just aiming for an abstract dream; you're building a roadmap for consistent effort and action. This structure helps you, as a leader, align your personal development with the broader objectives of your organization, serving both your growth and the collective mission.

Now, let's explore each element of the SMART acronym to better understand how it guides your commitment and ensures your consistency.

The goals need to be:

- **Specific:** A SMART goal is focused on a particular area of growth or expertise. Objectives are as narrow as possible. Pinpoint very specifically what you want to achieve rather than a general, vague, all-encompassing goal. If you're not specific enough, you won't know if you've actually achieved the goal—you need to drill it down to something very specific so you can be clear what you're measuring. Specificity includes establishing answers for who, what, when, where, why and how.
- **Measurable:** Your goal must be measurable so that you can track your progress and determine when you've achieved the end result. This includes establishing how many, how much, and by when.
- **Achievable:** Do you have the skill set, capability, or resources to complete the required work? Is it realistic? Is it possible to fit in your working life/personal lifestyle? A goal that is too big will have too many hurdles to overcome and steps to take, which makes it too easy to just procrastinate it away. By setting up an achievable goal, you'll know that you can reach it.
- **Relevant:** How does this goal relate to your life or work, and does it suit your own interests or where you

want to head in your career? The goal needs to apply to your current situation and long-term plans. This is usually by it improving some aspect of your work or job. How does the specific goal work to move you towards the bigger vision.

- **Time-bound:** Consider the time frame, including the start date and end date. One of the most critical metrics for achieving goals is timeliness. By setting up a deadline or endpoint, you have created the commitment to see the project through and achieve the goal. Putting a time constraint also allows you to gauge your progress throughout. Some goals will take a long time to complete, but it's best to stick to something more straightforward and immediate at the start. This will allow you to work actively on getting it done and enable you to course-correct if necessary.

Here's how that looks with my example of commitment to walking more in 2020.

- **Specific:** "I will walk at least five miles every day for my physical and mental health" instead of "I want to walk more."
- **Measurable:** "I will walk five miles daily and measure it on my smart watch."
- **Achievable:** "I have walked five miles before and have the fitness level and the time needed to do this."
- **Relevant:** "I value my physical and mental health and want to get out and walk more."
- **Time-bound:** "I want to do this until my birthday in three months' time" (which I completed, then extended the goal to keep going).

By looking at goals like this, you're essentially creating an action plan for something you want to accomplish. You create absolute clarity about what it is you're trying to achieve. And it's this clarity that gives you direction and the incentive to get going.

Now you try. Create a SMART goal around something important you want to change or achieve either personally or professionally. Make sure it fulfills each of the SMART elements.

## Follow One Course Until Successful (FOCUS)

After setting your SMART goals, the next hurdle is maintaining focus to see them through to completion. It's tempting to attempt huge, complex dream goals, but experience tells us that this is often a recipe for failure *if* you aren't fully prepared (more on that in a minute). The key in most instances is to start. Start with something that feels manageable and make incremental progress—small, consistent efforts that accumulate into meaningful transformation.

Imagine you've decided to introduce meditation or deep breathing into your daily routine. Rather than diving head-first into a week-long retreat or meditating for long, extended periods daily, start modestly. I usually have my clients either start with five minutes of deep breathing or a five-minute meditation track to start their day. This is a great first step. This may seem inconsequential, but its impact is two-fold: it's achievable and can be integrated into your routine without overwhelming you.

Allow for flexibility but aim for consistency. Over the course of two weeks, these daily 5-minute sessions will become a habit. You might find you want to extend the time as you become more comfortable, or maybe five minutes each day perfectly serves your needs. Either way, three months from now, the cumulative effect will be evident. You'll have cultivated a practice that enhances your mental clarity, without even realizing how far you've come.

This principle isn't limited to personal well-being; it can be applied universally across both your personal and professional life.

Here's a professional example:

Imagine you decide to improve your communication skills, particularly in the area of active listening (we'll discuss this topic more in Chapter 5). Rather than becoming overwhelmed by trying to take on several aspects of active listening, or trying to overhaul your entire communication style, you could start small. For example, you could decide that for all your one-to-one meetings with employees for the next month, you will practice giving the person you are speaking with your full attention. You would keep your phone and computer out of reach to avoid distractions. This goal aligns with the SMART framework: it's Specific, Measurable, Achievable, Relevant, and Time-Bound.

The practice of active listening serves two purposes: it helps you understand your team better because you are listening more carefully to what they are sharing with you, and it shows your team members that you value their input. And it's measurable; you can easily track whether you get distracted by your electronics in each meeting.

Just like the meditation example, the beauty of this approach is that it's incremental, you're practicing one skill in one kind of meeting, for one month. You'll soon find that active listening becomes almost second nature. Over time, this habit will not only improve your communication skills but also build trust and psychological safety within your team. Your team will see that you value their input.

# Create a multifaceted approach using a detailed plan

Let's say you decide to run the New York Marathon, and you're starting from a low baseline of physical fitness. Preparing for such a monumental undertaking is not something that should be done on a whim; it requires a thoughtful, multi-layered plan with a commitment to consistency, aligning well with the SMART goal framework.

You'd begin by defining your goal clearly—completing the marathon on the date set for that event. This goal is Specific, Measurable, and Time-Bound.

Next, you would assess the Achievability and Relevance of this goal. Is completing a marathon realistic given your current health and lifestyle? You ran a half-marathon a decade ago but have not run more than a 5k in years and you haven't run at all for a couple of years at least. How long is it likely to take you to get ready for this endeavor? Does this goal align with your broader objectives—perhaps a commitment to personal well-being, setting an example for your team or family, or even raising money for a good cause?

Now, the planning commences. You'd need to determine how many months are required for training, which is often around four to six months for a beginner or someone who hasn't run this distance in a long time. Within that timeline, you'll plan out weekly training sessions, incorporating varied types of workouts like long runs, interval training, and cross-training. You would also need to consider other key variables, like nutritional changes to support your training, and the gear you'll need—proper running shoes, clothing, and perhaps even a smartwatch to monitor your progress.

As you move forward, your commitment to this plan is your guide, and the consistency with which you execute each element helps to build momentum and a sense of accomplishment. This multifaceted approach also allows for assessment at various milestones. How are you doing? Are you being consistent? You might need to adjust your plan based on how your body is responding to the training or any unexpected challenges that arise, thus aligning with the continuous assessment aspect of SMART goals.

Training for a marathon is not merely an individual achievement but a demonstration of how setting a large, complex goal and breaking it down into achievable, realistic parts can lead to extraordinary outcomes. Moreover, the rigor and dedication required for such a feat make it a shining example for your team, showing that commitment and consistency can turn even the loftiest of goals into reality.

# Manage your time effectively

Imagine this: 81,396 hours, which equates to roughly nine years. At first glance, you may wonder what this number is related to? It's not the number of hours you spend sleeping in your lifetime (that's significantly more). And it's not the time it would take to travel to a distant planet. It is the average number of hours most individuals spend working in their lifetime, based on findings from a 2022 Gallup study.[10] Given this significant investment of our most valuable resource—time—it becomes imperative to consider how you spend your time at work.

Time management is the process of organizing and planning how to divide your time between specific activities—and not all of us are effective at it. Good time management enables you to work smarter—not harder—so that you get more done in less time, even when time is tight, and pressures are high. Being productive isn't ever about working more hours. It's about using your time wisely and efficiently to complete your work and meet deadlines.

Many people have significant problems with time management. It is one of the more frequent issues that come up for my clients and in my training sessions. The issues often include things like poor punctuality, poorly defined goals, procrastination, disorganization, lack of energy and commitment, and perfectionism. Oftentimes, they are feeling overwhelmed because there is so much work to do and they can't seem to get themselves organized enough to get things accomplished in a timely fashion. In contrast, those who can organize their time well are better able to meet deadlines, provide a higher quality of work, procrastinate less, experience less stress and anxiety, more opportunities for career growth, and have a better reputation. Most people would rather find themselves in the latter group than the former.

Can you see yourself in any of the types below?

- The Early Bird: The type of person who, when they get tasked with something, will immediately identify what needs doing and plan time accordingly. They usually get things done early and always arrive to meetings on time. They tend to prefer working on one thing at a time.

- The Multitasker: They like to get items on their to-do list done but tend to wait until the last minute—they like to switch their tasks up and work on multiple things at once. They often underestimate how long it will take to complete a task.
- The Helper: This person finds it hard to say no, and often will fall behind on their own work because they like to help others.
- The Deliberator: This person excels at breaking down large projects into individual tasks according to their priority and thrives on making decisions based on facts. They like to have enough time to review all information needed in any given task.

You can probably see that, of the above, those most effective for time management will likely be the "Early Bird" and the "Deliberator." Most people who think they are multitasking often come to realize that it's very difficult (bordering on impossible) to effectively give your full attention to more than one thing at a time. In the end, they feel scattered and overwhelmed with the tasks partially done.

One of the things that helps me is to sort tasks by each specific project, then decide which tasks can be done the fastest, and determine what needs more time.

Here are some time management techniques to help you get organized:

First, the *Pomodoro Technique,* a time management method developed by Francesco Cirillo in the late 1980s. You use a timer to break work or tasks into intervals, typically 25 minutes in length, separated by short breaks. After 25 minutes, take a break of around five minutes, then resume work. After four of those 25 five-minute cycles, take a 20-minute break. If you have a very short attention span, this is a great way to get yourself focused.

I often recommend *time blocking* (similar to Pomodoro) and *color coding* to my clients. Many of them find 25 minutes a bit short of a time period to work on a project. So what I suggest is that at the beginning of the week they plan out their tasks for the week and decide approximately how much time they need for the project for the week. Then block out chunks of time, no more than two hours at a time, to work on that task. So, if you determine that you need seven hours to complete a project this week, you will block out a two-hour block over three days and then one hour on the fourth day. The most important thing is to stick to the plan unless there is something *really urgent* you must attend to (see "Urgent–Important Matrix" below).

Most people's attention wanes after about an hour (the brain gets tired) so I recommend a quick five-minute change-of-state break. Use this time to stand up, stretch, have a bio break, get some water, go outside and get some fresh air, do jumping jacks, talk to a friend on the phone—whatever you want that gets you up and away from the computer. But only for five minutes. The goal is to shift your energy and refuel your brain to get focused again.

Color coding refers to using different colors in your calendar (on the computer or your phone) to identify different projects as well as time commitments in all areas of your life. You could choose a color for each large project you have so that you know which project you are working on when using your time blocks. On my calendar, I have one color for client appointments, a different color for general work meetings, I have another color for my personal responsibilities (including going to the gym) and still another for my daughter and other family responsibilities. It helps me know where I need to be and for whom.

Color coding and time blocking are very effective. However, one of the first things you need to do is figure out which things are really on your plate and what to give your attention to.

For this, use the Eisenhower Matrix, named after the 34th American President, Dwight D. Eisenhower, which is now more often called the *Time Management Matrix,* popularized by Stephen R. Covey in the book *The 7 Habits of Highly Effective People.*[11] It is in "Habit 3: Put First Things First." This tool is helpful for you to decide how to prioritize tasks by urgency and importance. This process may seem time-consuming at first; however, it will give you the opportunity to see whether you are spending your time on things that really help you and your team move things forward.

Get a piece of paper and divide it into four quadrants (see diagram). On the top left (Quadrant 1): write "Urgent and Important"; top right (Quadrant 2): "Not Urgent but Important"; on the bottom left (Quadrant 3): "Urgent but Not Important"; and then bottom right (Quadrant 4): "Not Urgent and Not Important".

Fill out the blocks with your tasks, depending on where they belong.

- Quadrant 1: crises, putting out fires, pressing problems, deadline-driven projects.
- Quadrant 2: prevention, relationship building, team development, proactive planning for future projects, seeking new opportunities.
- Quadrant 3: interruptions, some emails, pressing matters, many meetings.
- Quadrant 4: busy work, time wasters, scrolling social media, some phone calls, some meetings.

Be honest with yourself as you put things in their relevant quadrant. Be sure to include everything that takes up your time—even if it doesn't feel important. Once categorized, take a good look at how you spend much of your time. What are you doing most? Going to endless unimportant meetings? Or putting out the many fires or crises du jour?

Given your role, how best can you organize your time to ensure you allow for the important tasks, especially those that aren't urgent but are the proactive tasks that lead to better individual and team performance. Reschedule unimportant urgent tasks and avoid (if it's possible) tasks that are neither important nor urgent.

These techniques are more than organizational hacks; they're commitments to your well-being and the consistent, conscious choice to prioritize what truly matters and help you stay the course.

## APPLYING THE LEARNING

Based on what you've read in this chapter, ask yourself the following questions:

- What have you learned?
- What are your areas of growth?
- How will you apply your learnings from this chapter?

And then go a little deeper. Please be very specific.

- What two or three things are you going to start doing? _____
- What two or three things are you going to stop doing? _____
- What two or three things do you already do that you can continue doing? _____

## Self-Reflection Questions

1. What are my key commitments in my professional life, and how do I prioritize and demonstrate my dedication to these commitments on a daily basis?
2. How consistent is my performance at work, especially under varying circumstances? What factors contribute to my consistency, and how can I enhance it?
3. When facing obstacles or setbacks, how do I maintain my commitment to my tasks and goals? What strategies have I used in the past to stay focused and driven?

## Exercises

Complete the remaining Exercises 6–8 (pp. 193–4).

# PART 2

# Relationship Mastery: Cultivating the Skills of Connection

# 4

# Understanding Others: Mastering Social Awareness and Relationship Management

*Connection is the energy that exists between people when they feel seen, heard, and valued; when they can give and receive without judgment; and when they derive sustenance and strength from the relationship. Connection is why we're here; we are hardwired to connect with others; it's what gives purpose and meaning to our lives.*

BRENÉ BROWN

As Brené Brown so eloquently captures in the quote above, the essence of human interaction lies in connection. It is the fuel that drives our relationships. Neuroscience research confirms that our brains are hardwired for social connections.[12] When we interact with others, specific neurons—known as mirror neurons—become active in our brain. These neurons essentially "light up" neural pathways that resonate with the emotions and behaviors expressed by the person we're engaging with.

For leaders, this sense of connection isn't a nice-to-have—it's the heart of effective leadership. As we move forward from the first part of this book, where I emphasized the importance of understanding yourself through self-awareness and self-management, we arrive at the next key point: how to understand others and master relationships. In this chapter, we will delve into the two remaining pillars of emotional intelligence—social awareness and relationship management.

To be an influential leader, you need to excel not just in understanding yourself, but also in understanding the people you work with—their wants, needs, desires, feelings, thoughts, dreams, and goals. Your leadership style should reflect a holistic view that incorporates an awareness of what's occurring both within you and around you. Simply put, effective leadership goes beyond the "I" and deeply engages with the "we." Cultivating those skills of connection and managing interpersonal relationships correctly will help you continue on your path of growth as a leader. Because leadership is all about guiding and influencing others.

Social awareness complements self-awareness, as Daniel Goleman shared in his book, *Emotional Intelligence: Why It Can Matter More Than IQ* (1995).[13] It's about how you perceive the emotions of others, recognize social cues, and interpret them accurately. This skill forms the foundation for relationship management, the fine art of developing strong bonds, defusing conflicts, and nurturing a collaborative environment.

Consider for a moment the flip side: what happens when a leader lacks proficiency in social awareness and relationship management? A deficit in these areas doesn't merely result in minor hiccups—it often leads to systemic dysfunction within the team and can impact the organization. When a leader fails to understand their team, misreads situations, or misses social cues, the ramifications are substantial. Not only do misunderstandings become more frequent, but conflict often becomes the norm rather than the exception.

In such an environment, morale deteriorates rapidly. Team members may become disengaged, skeptical of leadership, and less willing to take the extra step to ensure a project's success. The absence of emotional intelligence at the leadership level can stifle innovation and collaboration, as employees become more cautious and less willing to share their ideas openly. Ultimately, this diminishes both productivity and the overall well-being of the team. A leader who can't effectively manage interpersonal relationships risks cultivating a culture where trust is scarce, and fear or apathy prevails. This is a far cry from the mutual respect and effective teamwork that are the goals of successful teams and organizations.

It's essential to ask yourself: how can we work together, better?

The goal here is to enrich your understanding of others which will ultimately enable you to construct a framework of mutual respect and effective teamwork.

# NEURODIVERSE AND NEUROTYPICAL BRAINS

Although neurodiversity is increasingly recognized in today's world, it's often overlooked in traditional leadership training. Neurodiversity describes the natural variations in human brain function and behavior that deviate from what is considered "neurotypical" or the societal norm. It reflects the diversity of human cognition and references a wide range of neurological differences, including but not limited to dyslexia, attention deficit hyperactivity disorder (ADHD), dyspraxia, autism, and Tourette's syndrome, among others.

Neurodivergent individuals may process information, communicate, and interact with the world in unique ways that diverge from the majority. These neurological differences are often associated with distinct cognitive strengths and challenges.

Understanding this distinction is crucial for leaders aiming to create an inclusive work environment, as neurodivergent individuals may experience the workplace—and particularly social interactions—differently than their neurotypical counterparts.

Even for a neurotypical brain, mastering social cues and awareness is challenging. When you add neurodiversity to the mix, it becomes an even more nuanced endeavor. Neurodivergent individuals might perceive social cues differently, making traditional methods of leadership less effective or even counterproductive. These methods often rely heavily on social cues, unwritten norms, and indirect communication, which can be problematic for neurodivergent individuals.

This presents an interesting challenge for leaders: how do you create a culture of inclusivity and belonging when the conventional methods of social interaction may not be universally understood?

Herein lies the importance of flexibility and adaptation. Adhering strictly to traditional approaches without considering the needs and strengths of neurodivergent individuals can be limiting and may even create unnecessary barriers to their success and inclusion within the team. As a leader, you have to be willing to incorporate diverse communication styles and different ways of learning or interacting to be more effective and inclusive.

First, it's important to be knowledgeable but not make assumptions. While it's useful to understand the challenges that individuals with ADHD or autism might face, such as difficulty with focus or social interactions, remember that neurodivergent individuals are not a monolithic group. Each person will have their unique strengths and challenges. Therefore, being educated on neurodivergence should not translate into making assumptions or stereotyping team members.

Neurodiversity can significantly enhance a workplace in several ways. Neurodivergent workers often contribute an edge in innovation and creativity, bringing technical, design, and creative strengths that enrich the collective skill set. They may approach problem-solving from novel angles, offering alternative solutions that might otherwise be overlooked. Some individuals exhibit high levels of concentration, keen accuracy, and an uncanny ability to detect errors—qualities that are invaluable in any professional setting. Additionally, their strong recall of information and detailed factual knowledge can be instrumental in complex tasks. These attributes, along with their reliability and persistence, mean neurodivergent employees can make excellent team members.

I should also note that some of the most innovative and successful entrepreneurs and leaders in the business world identify as neurodivergent.[14] Richard Branson, founder of

Virgin Atlantic; Daymond John, founder and CEO of FUBU and Investor on *Shark Tank*; Charles Schwab, founder and Chairman of Charles Schwab Corporation; Ingvar Kamprad, founder of IKEA; David Neeleman, founder of JetBlue; and Barbara Corcoran, founder of the Corcoran Group and Investor on *Shark Tank*—all with ADHD and/or dyslexia— are prime examples. So is Elon Musk, founder of Tesla, who has Asperger's. Their neurodivergence has not been a barrier but rather a catalyst for creative problem-solving and disruptive innovation.

Some neurodivergent employees and leaders may need support, but there cannot be a one-size-fits-all approach to accommodation as needs vary.

Examples may include:

- Flexible schedules.
- A quiet work environment.
- Regular check-ins.
- Access to mental health support.
- Clear and structured communication.
- Modifying expectations around social interactions.

One simple change could be offering multiple ways to engage through written communication, one-on-one meetings, or group brainstorming sessions. This approach not only accommodates neurodivergent individuals but also caters to diverse learning and communication styles within your team.

An essential strategy is cultivating an environment where team members feel safe to disclose their needs without fear of repercussion. While you may not know for sure whether someone is neurodivergent, creating an open environment can make it easier for people to share what they need to succeed. This psychological safety is an integral part of any team's success, regardless of neurodiversity.

Promoting self-awareness (as we discussed in Chapter 1) can also be a crucial step. By encouraging team members to recognize their emotional triggers or patterns, you're not only helping neurodivergent individuals but also creating a more emotionally intelligent team overall.

While your neurodivergent team members may need some accommodations, it's vital for leaders to also recognize the unique skills and talents they bring to the team.

Remember, creating a culture of inclusion benefits everyone, not just those who are neurodivergent. Whether or not you're aware of the specific neurodivergences within your team, these inclusive practices contribute to an environment where everyone feels seen, heard, and valued.

## DEVELOPING YOUR SOCIAL AWARENESS SKILLS

At the beginning of my doctoral journey, whenever I told people that I was studying psychology, they would often ask, "Are you analyzing me?" For a long time, my answer was, "No! Of course not!" But over the years I have come to realize that actually, yes, I do… kind of. You see, I don't see it as something that I actively do—analyze people. However, I do have very heightened observation skills and my curiosity is at a very high level, so I generally notice things that most people do not. My brain is constantly scanning people and the environment for clues as to what is going on and how people are doing. It isn't something I can switch on and off. It is just who I am. It gives me a great ability to connect with people, notice when someone might be in trouble and need some assistance, and be levelheaded in a crisis.

While my heightened observation skills and acute sense of curiosity are traits that have undoubtedly enriched my understanding of human behavior and contributed to my success as a professional, you don't have to hold a doctorate in psychology to cultivate these traits. They are skills that can—and should—be developed by everyone, especially leaders. Tuning into the subtle nuances of people's behavior, their tone, and even their choice of words can offer invaluable insights into what drives them, what concerns them, and how they are likely to react in different situations.

Why is this important for leaders? Because to be a great leader it is important to have the ability to understand others, to anticipate their needs, and to respond in a way that furthers both individual and collective goals. And here's the rub: understanding others is not just about being perceptive; it's also about being receptive. It's about being the one who can create a safe space where your team feels seen, heard, and valued—reaffirming the words of Brené Brown that opened this chapter.

You can work to improve social awareness in many different ways—and this includes considering body language, practicing empathy in your conversations—stepping into someone else's shoes, and challenging your biases.

## Pay attention to body language

What do you notice about people? Are you able to tell how someone is feeling by the expression on their face? Do you stand very close to people when you are speaking to them or give them at least an arm's length of space?

Body language is an essential component of human interaction, so much so that research by Dr. Albert Mehrabian reveals that 55% of communication is nonverbal (we'll discuss more about his startling statistics in Chapter 5).[15] By paying attention to body language, you have invaluable access to a wealth of information that may often reveal sentiments that aren't expressed verbally. Whether it's a fleeting glance or a slight shift in posture, these can serve as a barometer for the emotional climate of a room, thereby enabling you to adapt your communication strategy more effectively.

Facial expressions often serve as a window into an individual's emotional state. A furrowed brow or a smile can speak volumes, allowing you to gauge team morale or identify unspoken concerns. Similarly, understanding the intricacies of personal space and physical boundaries can prevent misunderstandings and promote a sense of respect among team members. Being sensitive to these nonverbal cues can ensure that your employees feel more comfortable. Gestures, too, are an element of nonverbal communication to mindfully observe. A simple nod can affirm that a message has been understood, while a dismissive wave may indicate disinterest or disagreement.

Your challenge here is not only to notice these nonverbal cues, but to interpret them accurately, and it can get tricky. Consider behaviors like arm folding, often misconstrued as defensiveness or disinterest. In reality, this could be a person's natural stance or even a means to comfort themselves. Whenever I speak about this in a training, I often get pushback from people who say that they sit with their arms folded because it is just how they sit. They aren't thinking about how this behavior is being misinterpreted. The same is true for fidgeting and doodling in meetings—actions frequently labeled as signs of disengagement or restlessness. However, numerous people, including those who are neurodivergent, find that these activities enhance their focus and listening skills. Thus, it's imperative to resist making snap judgments based on isolated behavioral cues. When confronted with ambiguous signals, seek clarity through open dialogue.

The key point there is realizing that nonverbal communication speaks volumes. As a leader, take the time to observe what is happening around you and be curious as to what those facial expressions or gestures might mean. Body language offers a nuanced, layered context that, when interpreted thoughtfully, enriches your effectiveness and team culture.

## Become an active listener

Active listening provides the basis for genuine human connection and cohesive collaboration. Being socially aware isn't just about observing others; it's about deeply understanding them. Better listening skills will elevate the quality of your interactions by allowing you to perceive not just what is being said, but how it is said, including the unspoken emotional context.

While many people assume they are good listeners, the reality is that true listening is more intricate than merely hearing words. Active listening involves a mental commitment to understand not just the content but the emotional subtext of what someone is saying.

For leaders, this skill will equip you to respond empathically and make informed decisions that take into account the dynamics of your team.

Consider this scenario: one of your employees opens up in your one-to-one about feeling overwhelmed with their workload. Your usual response might be to offer a solution immediately or perhaps share a story of when you, too, have felt overwhelmed and how you solved it. But when practicing active listening, it may be helpful to pause, absorbing not just the words but the stress and concern behind them. This will allow you to respond in a way that validates the employee's feelings and signals that they've been heard and understood. When you are able to consistently demonstrate this level of understanding, your employees will more likely feel like they can fully express themselves without fear of judgment.

Active listening is not just about the words you hear; it's about observing body language, recognizing the tone, and even noting what is not being said. It's a practice of piecing together multiple cues to grasp an accurate understanding of the situation. For example, if you notice someone's vocal tone doesn't match their words—"I'm fine," said with a sigh—you're using active listening to pick up on that discrepancy.

While we will explore more deeply the process of active listening in the next chapter, remember for now that the power of active listening extends beyond solving problems; it's about building relationships that are based on mutual understanding and respect.

## Step into their shoes

Empathic listening is an extension of active listening but goes deeper, focusing on emotional resonance and understanding. While active listening might involve fully comprehending the spoken words and their immediate context, empathic listening pushes us to explore the emotional landscape the person speaking might be navigating. Imagine someone tells you they've just been laid off. Rather than just hearing these as facts, empathic listening would prompt you to consider the emotional weight behind those words. How would you feel if you were in their position (given their exact circumstances not your current ones)? What kind of support would you desire from your colleagues or friends?

The power of empathic listening lies in its ability to cultivate deeper, more meaningful connections. It goes beyond preventing misunderstandings; it helps you respond with both understanding and compassion. When you practice this advanced form of listening, you can better discern not just what team members are trying to communicate, but also grasp the emotional texture of their experiences.

## Seek the whole picture

In our fast-paced work environments, it's easy to jump to conclusions based on incomplete information. But if you want to truly understand a situation, you need to collect insights from multiple sources. Let's say you observe a colleague who's stressed because their manager pressured them about a looming deadline. It's tempting to immediately label the manager as overly demanding. But have you considered the chain of pressures the manager might also be facing? Perhaps there's urgency from the client's end, or maybe the manager has targets to meet to secure funding for the next quarter.

By viewing a situation from multiple angles, you're not only giving yourself a fuller understanding, but you're also setting the stage for more effective problem-solving. So before making judgments, take a step back. Speak with different stakeholders involved in the issue or gather perspectives from those who have been in similar situations. This holistic approach will help you make more informed decisions and less inaccurate assumptions.

# Challenge your biases

In Chapter 2, we discussed how the inherent biases that influence our thinking also impact our decisions and actions. As we build upon those foundational insights, it's crucial to understand how these biases specifically impact our capacity for social awareness in leadership roles.

Unconscious biases are like invisible scripts that run continuously in the background of our minds. They are formed by our upbringing, our experiences, and societal influences, culminating in a set of assumptions that govern our interactions with others. While these biases might have helped our ancestors quickly assess friend from enemy, in today's nuanced world, they can severely impede our ability to make fair judgments and decisions. Especially in leadership roles, where impartiality is crucial, being attuned to our own biases is paramount.

Understanding the roots of our biases often starts with self-examination. If, for example, you notice you're more attentive to certain voices during meetings or more likely to assign challenging projects to individuals of a particular background, you're observing your biases in action. Your brain takes shortcuts, creating a narrative based on limited information. In doing so, it reinforces existing stereotypes, perpetuating a cycle that can be damaging both personally and professionally.

One practical approach to countering this is to adopt a "second thought" strategy. Whenever you make an initial judgment or decision, pause for a moment and consider whether it's influenced by a bias. Challenge your first thought, question what caused you to come up with that particular one, and then actively consider more options. Once you have reflected on a variety of options, and perhaps sought counsel from others, make a reasoned, balanced choice. This creates an opportunity to break the cycle of unconscious bias and bring more nuanced thinking to your decision-making process. None of this is to say that your initial thoughts are always going to be inherently wrong. But it is important to be very clear as to the basis of your decisions, and to ensure they aren't rooted in bias.

In leadership, this level of awareness has ripple effects. By continually examining and owning your biases, you open the door to becoming a more socially aware leader. Challenging your preconceived notions isn't just an intellectual exercise; it's a responsibility. When you turn that mirror towards yourself and interrogate your own thinking, you're enriching your own perspective and also setting the stage for others to feel safe to do the same.

# ORGANIZATIONAL AWARENESS

As you continue to build social awareness, it's crucial not to overlook the importance of organizational awareness, which is one of the 12 components of social awareness in Daniel Goleman's framework of emotional intelligence.[16] It refers to the ability to understand the social fabric within an organization—the dynamics, power structures, unspoken rules, and even the emotional undercurrents. A leader with high organizational awareness is attuned to the overall vibe or culture of the workplace and can effectively navigate or influence it.

This skill becomes invaluable for driving change, fostering collaboration, and influencing key stakeholders. Leaders who possess organizational awareness can gauge not only how decisions are made but also who the influential players are, what they value, and how to engage them. Moreover, organizational awareness allows you to anticipate challenges, understand resistance, and see beyond surface-level issues to the root causes that affect productivity and employee well-being. In a nutshell, organizational awareness equips leaders to act in a way that is most congruent with the organization's goals and values while also being sensitive to its human elements.

You can start building on this set of skills by conducting regular check-ins across different levels of the organization. It can be enlightening. These conversations provide a pulse check on the organizational mood and reveal underlying dynamics that may not be immediately obvious.

It will also be important to be present in various settings—be it team meetings or all-hands sessions so you are present and can make contributions. While you're there, don't just focus on the spoken words. Take note of the subtleties (as we discussed earlier in this chapter), such as how things are said and what remains unspoken. Also, keep an eye on internal communications like newsletters and memos, as they often reflect the organization's priorities and challenges. By adopting these practices, you'll develop a more nuanced understanding of your organization's culture and power dynamics.

## STRONG RELATIONSHIPS MAKE FOR HAPPIER, MORE ENGAGED WORKPLACES

Relationship management serves as the culmination of all the elements of emotional intelligence. It embodies the practical application of self-awareness, self-regulation, and social awareness in relational interactions. You empower, inspire, and elevate others and develop strong interpersonal relationships by utilizing your skills and awareness effectively.

While your team may not be a family (and shouldn't be treated as one), the relationships within it are critically important. A positive, respectful work atmosphere can significantly improve your well-being and job satisfaction. This is particularly crucial during times of stress, which, as we know, is an inevitable part of any work environment.

Individuals with high emotional intelligence skills can manage their stress and anger more efficiently when conflicts arise. They approach problems calmly, without projecting their frustrations onto others, focusing instead on maintaining peace, finding solutions, and encouraging collaboration. It is vital to understand that the effective use of these emotional intelligence skills not only nurtures a positive work atmosphere but also serves as a powerful deterrent against the emergence of a toxic work environment.

So often I hear stories of managers belittling their employees, micromanaging their every moment, or dismissing their contributions in meetings. It causes such distress, leading to physical and emotional well-being problems. Survey after survey confirm that this area—how people treat each other at work—isn't going well.

And *you* can do something about it.

Strong interpersonal relationships lay the foundation for effective teams, promoting an atmosphere where employees feel respected and valued. This respect becomes the anchor for openness, making it easier for team members to share new ideas, contribute meaningfully, and work well together.

If you can master relationship management, you're not just enhancing your own work experience. You're setting a standard and cultivating an environment where everyone can collaborate effectively, solve problems creatively, and contribute to the organization's success.

Beyond continuing to work on yourself and all the skills described in the previous chapters of this book, take an interest in the individual and collective growth of your team. What new technical, professional, or soft skills would help them thrive? They have unique aspirations and skills that, when nurtured, benefit not only them but the whole group. By providing mentorship opportunities or even something as simple as recommending a good read, you send the message that you care about them as people.

Work together to build a team culture that appreciates every small win while constructively addressing setbacks; it will add an extra layer of cohesion and camaraderie within the team. When you celebrate successes and view setbacks as learning opportunities (without placing blame), they will develop resilience and problem-solving skills.

It's worth noting that the effective application of these emotional intelligence skills plays a vital role in preventing a toxic work environment. Leaders attuned to both their own emotions and those of others are well positioned to defuse conflicts early and establish a culture of respect and inclusion.

## WORKING WITH DIFFICULT PEOPLE—AND THE NEED FOR CIVILITY

A huge source of stress at work is the need to adjust to different personalities. Each person is unique, and even when you're dealing with a responsible and emotionally mature co-worker, friction is inevitable simply because the other person will never be exactly like you.

When you share a workspace with others, differences in habits, communication styles, and preferences are inevitable. While many of these differences can be accommodated through mutual respect and understanding, the challenge escalates when you're dealing with someone who exhibits what can generally be characterized as a "difficult" personality.

The notion of what makes a personality "difficult" is obviously quite subjective and varies from person to person. However, people perceived as particularly difficult are often those who manifest *inflexible extremes* of personality traits. This lack of adaptability can escalate everyday interactions into stressful or confrontational encounters.

Take, for example, the issue of control in managerial positions. A certain degree of control is not just beneficial but necessary for effective management. However, there's a fine line between exercising appropriate control and excessive micromanagement. I have heard from many employees that excessive control has eroded trust within teams, stifling their creativity, and leading to a decline in overall team functioning.

Similarly, an overly consultative approach can also prove problematic. While it's commendable to seek the opinions of colleagues on key decisions, an extreme need for consultation or consensus can be masking dependency issues. This not only hampers the decision-making process but can also

strain professional relationships, making this colleague difficult to work alongside.

Our default reactions to these difficult personalities often
exacerbate the problem rather than solve it. Whether it's
avoiding or being confrontational with a dominant personality, lecturing someone who's overly dependent, or retaliating
against passive-aggressive behavior, these coping mechanisms
are typically counterproductive. They are not going to help
and will perpetuate a cycle of dysfunctional interactions that
only further entrench the difficulties at hand.

The better option may be to focus on setting a standard
of civility.

Civility is one of the best ways to deal with difficult personalities in the workplace.

It sets the stage for effective communication—in many
ways, dealing with difficult personalities is simply a matter
of setting and negotiating boundaries. After all, difficult personalities are not "bad people." They just have a fixed way
of relating and may simply require constructive feedback to
adapt their communication style.

As a leader, one of your roles includes mitigating workplace incivility to cultivate a cooperative and effective organizational climate. Incivility can be caused by a variety of
factors such as a lack of self-awareness, stress, neurodiverse
differences, competition, or cultural differences.

Adopting civil conduct creates a welcoming environment,
allowing for a deeper understanding of the underlying motivations behind people's actions. What one might label as a
difficult personality could merely be a colleague with unmet
needs or unresolved issues, whether it's a desire for recognition for their work efforts or displaced emotional distress
from personal matters.

By choosing to act courteously with colleagues, you're setting the stage for empathic and supportive exchanges. This,
in turn, paves the way for more constructive interactions, mitigating the challenges that come with difficult personalities.

Practicing civility gives you a framework for productive
and respectful collaboration. The term "civility" often evokes

notions of respect, politeness, tolerance, thoughtfulness, and rational conflict resolution. Embracing these norms as a team equips each person with skills that extend well beyond the workplace.

## MAINTAINING POSITIVE RELATIONSHIPS IN THE WORKPLACE

Civility is at the core of maintaining healthy, respectful, relationships in the workplace… but how else can you work to improve your relationships with colleagues?

Here are four additional points worth considering:

1. *Be open and curious.*
   If you find yourself in a conflict at work, don't make assumptions or jump to conclusions. Ask questions. Analyze what happened. Listen to different points of view. This requires you to draw on social awareness strategies and challenge your own biases to be open and curious about the situation.

2. *Practice good manners.*
   Simplicity can go far in managing your relationships. Manners are important—sometimes a missed apology, or even a missed "hello," can be misinterpreted. Strive to always be kind, compassionate, and polite.

3. *Avoid mixed signals.*
   Relationship management skills don't fare well with mixed messaging or signals. Being clear with the words you say, as well as your body language, is important.

4. *Communicate effectively.*
   Communication couldn't be more important in these situations. What words you use, how you say them,

and who you say them to can impact how you are perceived. We'll explore communication more in the next chapter.

## PUTTING THESE COMPONENTS INTO ACTION

Honing your skills in social awareness and relationship management not only elevates your rapport with employees and colleagues, but it also establishes the framework for connections that are mutually beneficial. This becomes a catalyst for effective networking—a critical asset in both your professional and personal life.

Networking unlocks new opportunities and serves as a conduit for the free flow of ideas and creativity. Within an organizational context, this enables career advancement and propels individuals closer to their personal and professional goals. Moreover, effective networking can amplify your industry reputation and visibility, thereby advancing your career path.

In this chapter, we've laid the foundation for Part 2—focusing on building connections through authentic and resilient relationships. By now I hope you have a better understanding the complexities of emotional intelligence and how to better navigate the nuances of interpersonal dynamics.

## APPLYING THE LEARNING

Based on what you've read in this chapter, ask yourself the following questions:

- What have you learned?
- What are your areas of growth?
- How will you apply your learnings from this chapter?

And then go a little deeper. Please be very specific.

- What two or three things are you going to start doing? _____
- What two or three things are you going to stop doing? _____
- What two or three things do you already do that you can build on? _____

## Self-Reflection Questions

1. How well do I understand the social dynamics and relationships within my team and the wider organization? In what ways have I actively worked to improve my understanding and navigate these dynamics more effectively?

2. How do my actions and decisions impact the people around me in the workplace? Can I recall a recent instance where I adjusted my approach based on the needs or reactions of others?

3. How do I ensure that my interactions with colleagues, regardless of the situation, are conducted with civility and respect? Can I identify any recent instances where I could have been more civil, and what could I have done differently?

4. What common triggers or situations lead to conflict in my workplace (on my team), and how have I, as a leader, contributed to these situations? What proactive steps can I take in the future to anticipate and mitigate these conflict triggers in the future?

# 5

# Beyond Words: The Nuances of Powerful Communication

*Communication makes the world go round. It facilitates human connections, and allows us to learn, grow and progress. It's not just about speaking or reading, but understanding what is being said—and in some cases what is not being said. Being able to effectively communicate is the most important skill any leader can possess.*

RICHARD BRANSON

Communication is not merely an exchange between people; it's an intricate dance that involves much more than words alone. It's a multifaceted endeavor often underestimated and misunderstood, despite its crucial role in the success or failure of interpersonal relationships and team dynamics.

The interesting thing I have observed is that most people consider themselves to be "good to great" communicators and yet frequently find themselves in misunderstandings and interpersonal conflict. They often believe the communication issue to be "the other person's problem" without being curious about how they might contribute to it.

According to the *Merriam-Webster Dictionary*, communication is the art of "exchanging, expressing, or conveying information and ideas through writing, speaking, and gesturing." While this definition provides a basis for understanding, it only scratches the surface of the breadth and depth of what communication truly entails.

One prevalent misconception is that communication is primarily about the words we use. In fact, according to the 7-38-55 rule coined by Dr. Albert Mehrabian (as mentioned in Chapter 4), a mere 7% of communication consists of the words we speak.[17] The tonality of our voice accounts for 38%, and 55% is conveyed through body language and facial expressions. We cannot dismiss the importance of these key elements. While words are the framework upon which we build our intentions, they are not the entire structure. In business, for example, a well-crafted email might convey a point, but it's the ensuing face-to-face meeting, the tone used when speaking during a conference call, or even the timing of a message that can seal the deal—or break it.

But the complexities of communication do not end there. Most people assume that all of our listening skills are honed during our early years at school. And, while it's true that we're introduced to basic techniques for absorbing and processing information early on, genuine listening—being able to listen without judgment or interruption, with the intent to understand rather than simply respond—is a lifelong endeavor. These are critical skills that most of us (including me) still strive to refine, irrespective of our age or level of experience.

For leaders, in particular, the stakes are high. Your ability to communicate clearly and listen attentively is essential for building trust not only with your immediate team and senior leaders but also with a diverse set of stakeholders. This includes cross-functional teams, clients, suppliers, board members, regulatory agencies, investors, and even the community at large. The spectrum of people leaders must effectively communicate with is wide-ranging, each requiring a nuanced approach to establish trust and facilitate meaningful interaction.

So, in this chapter, we will unpack the nuances that make communication both an art and a science. We'll explore both the mechanics and the psychology behind effective communication, because understanding the "how" is meaningless without grasping the "why." We must remember that meaningful interaction bridges the gap between individuals and leads to connection.

## COMMUNICATION CHALLENGES

Poor communication is a pervasive issue that affects people in many environments, especially workplaces. If you're struggling with it—on either side of the interaction—you're far from alone. Based on my own observations from my clients and organizational trainings, it seems that many people, leaders in particular, aren't aware that their communication skills need work. And, according to an Interact/Harris survey, a staggering 91% of 1,000 employees identified a "lack of critical communication skills" among leaders.[18] The survey also uncovered that 57% of respondents cited "unclear directions" as the most common communication barrier. In a separate Interact/Harris survey of 2058 adults, 69% of respondents who were managers admitted feeling "uncomfortable" when communicating with employees.[19] There is clearly work to do here.

Clear communication is necessary for goal achievement. It mitigates confusion, bestows purpose, and creates account-ability. While the formula for effective communication seems straightforward—a clear message is sent and accurately received and then expectations are met—the reality is more complex. Several factors act as obstacles to this ideal, some of which have been discussed earlier in this book.

## HOW YOU DEVELOP MALADAPTIVE COMMUNICATION HABITS

Many people develop maladaptive habits that interfere with effective communication. Recognizing that these habits exist is the first step towards unlearning them, a process that involves both awareness and continuous practice.

(Side note—I prefer to substitute the words "mal-adaptive" or "unhelpful" for the word "bad" because they better capture the complexities of communication habits that are not effective. "Maladaptive" habits are behaviors that, although perhaps developed as coping mechanisms or shortcuts, are ultimately detrimental to effective communication and personal growth. Similarly, "unhelpful" underscores that the habit may not contribute to your goals or the team's well-being. The word "bad" isn't constructive and is often used to pass judgment on ourselves and others.)

One maladaptive habit to really take notice of is how stereotypes and generalizations may reside in your daily communication, without you noticing. Over 90% of our thoughts occur subconsciously, often leading us to make snap automatic judgments about people based on our conditioned biases. These judgments affect how we engage, speak to, and communicate with others. For example, you could have a bias against people with high-pitched voices, who don't look at you directly when they are speaking to you, or who have clammy hands when they shake your hand. Or you may think that people with curly or afro hair or tattoos or a nose piercing look unprofessional. Although these may not seem important, these "silly" biases could easily get in the way of someone being hired or promoted if the hiring manager had biases against people with these characteristics. The same is true for more significant biases that are based on race, ethnicity, gender, age, religion, disability, and LGBTQ+. When you aren't paying attention to how your biases affect your communication and decision-making, you run the risk of those biases creating an uncomfortable, at a minimum, or toxic, at its worst, environment for your team.

There are currently five generations active in the workforce: the Silent Generation—born between 1928 and 1945; Baby Boomers—born between 1946 and 1964; Gen X—born between 1965 and 1980; Millennials—born between 1981 and 1996; and Gen Z—born between 1997 and 2012.[20] Each generation brings different backgrounds, mindsets, and expectations to the workplace. It has become easy to stick a stereotype label on each large group. Understandably, each generation is uniquely different as their life experiences and the generational culture they grew up in is very different. But what I have been noticing, in my trainings, is that there is a lot of ageist stereotyping.

For example, Boomers and Gen Xers flatly refusing to have a Millennial be their manager simply because they are "too young to know anything." Or Gen X leaders stating that "these young people just have to learn how to take orders and stop getting in their feelings. They are so difficult to work with and they don't know the value of hard work." As a younger psychologist, I remember dealing with other people's biases, with them saying to me, "You don't look like a psychologist" or "You're too young to know anything." I've always wondered exactly what a psychologist is supposed to look like. Millennials often stereotype Boomers and Gen Xers as inflexible, rigid, and resistant to change. "They aren't interested in new ideas or innovation; they won't even listen to my ideas. And anything tech related, they just aren't interested in learning about it."

These are biases. These lenses shape your view of large groups who may share certain traits among themselves but differ from you. Such biases and stereotypes can adversely influence both your perception of and engagement with team members who share commonality with other groups. It becomes essential, then, to continually examine your own potential biases.

Ask yourself, "Are my perspectives about this person free from bias?" And don't immediately assume that they are. Sit with the question for a while and reflect. If we use the example above, do you make comments, generalizations, or jokes about people from other generations in meetings? Millennials are... GenXers are... Gen Z is... Is it possible your comments, a form of communication, might have a negative impact on the people hearing you? Something to think about. Get feedback from others, be brave and ask people who are different whether or not your communications and decisions are free from bias. This exercise will help you identify some of the biases in your communication and, armed with this new awareness, you have a choice to make—evolve or stay the same.

And when you discover that there is room for improvement, consider revisiting Chapter 2 to understand the origins of these biases and how to shift them. This self-awareness is a crucial step in deliberately shedding any conditioning that might stand in the way of cultivating an inclusive work environment with your team.

Listening may not seem like it could be a "maladaptive habit," but so many people just aren't really listening. Hearing itself is a passive act—assuming an individual is not hearing-impaired, hearing simply happens. But listening is an essential, active component of meaningful dialogue. It is a choice. We have touched on active listening in Chapters 3 and 4 and will explore it in more depth later in this chapter.

Your personality can also be a barrier to how well you communicate with someone. It's quite common to meet people with very different personalities from your own on your team and in your organization. How well do you relate to and communicate with people who are significantly different from you? If they are more or less outgoing, quiet, organized?

Each person you encounter will have a unique communication style. Some people prefer a more direct, straightforward, cut-to-the-chase communication style. Others must get all the details to fully understand what you mean. Still others communicate with more emotion and want to understand the bigger mission or purpose. They will also have preferences for *how* to be communicated with. While some might prefer a brief email directive or a quick Teams Instant Message, others might require a detailed phone conversation or face-to-face meeting to understand their tasks fully. A one-size-fits-all strategy is bound to leave some people confused and others disengaged.

I do always recommend to my clients that they should send an email to confirm instructions, because many people don't listen very well to details and miss very important pieces in conversations about projects with deadlines and deliverables. As the leader, you will believe you have explained your expectations fully, and they will say they don't have clarity. Oftentimes, we just ask people, "Do you understand?" and I have personally often experienced that people will say, "Yes," but have no idea what you are talking about! And while I agree that it is also the responsibility of the person who is listening to ask questions and seek to understand, the reality is that there are many reasons, including a power imbalance that may have employees not wanting to appear "dumb" (this is how they describe it), and so they nod their head and say they understand. As the leader, ask open-ended questions, have them explain the project or task instructions back to you, or send you an email outlining their understanding. Then you can "confirm" that there is clarity and understanding.

Also, recognize that it's practically impossible to have a productive conversation when you're not in the best emotional state or being impulsive. If you are very stressed, angry, disappointed, or upset, your feelings will influence your tone, words, and body language. This can get in the way, confuse things, or even shut down communication altogether. It isn't appropriate in any setting, but especially not at work, to inflict your negative emotions on other people. Being aware of how your emotions and behavior impact how you talk to others and recognizing the necessity of keeping your impulses in check is key to having better conversations. Take the time to calm yourself down, take some deep breaths, or go for a walk instead of having conversations in a heightened emotional state.

# WHAT IS EFFECTIVE COMMUNICATION?

A highly skilled communicator embodies multiple capabilities. First and foremost, they actively engage in two-way dialogue, facilitating conversations that allow both parties to express their viewpoints openly. This may sound easy, but it isn't. Giving both people ample time to make their point creates an atmosphere of mutual respect, where everyone involved feels heard and valued. But active participation goes beyond just talking—it means being an active listener. Adept communicators don't merely hear the words; they understand the underlying emotions, context, and nuances.

Effective communicators also navigate the tone of the conversation with finesse. They refrain from using sarcasm or any form of communication that could potentially cause conflict. Their tone is amicable yet professional, creating an environment conducive for open, honest, and transparent dialogue. Trust is at the forefront of their interactions; they understand that the words they choose and the manner in which they are delivered can either build trust or erode it.

Deep listening is another hallmark of an effective communicator. They aren't simply waiting for their turn to speak, but fully engage with what is being said. This enables them to respond with empathy, taking into consideration not just the content but also the emotional context of the conversation. Their understanding of interpersonal dynamics is refined, allowing them to adapt their communication style to different colleagues, issues, and situations.

How well we communicate is central to our personal and professional success. When we communicate well, we are better able to build stronger relationships. Effective communication enriches our understanding, helping us discover new facets of projects or ideas that we might not have considered otherwise. Furthermore, it facilitates personal and professional growth, opening avenues for us to acquire essential information and knowledge.

> *Leadership is communicating to people their worth and potential so clearly that they come to see it in themselves.*
> STEPHEN R. COVEY

## What you say

While Mehrabian's rule suggests that only 7% of communication is rooted in the words we use, the power of that 7% shouldn't be underestimated. The words we choose to verbalize our thoughts and expectations have a tremendous impact on our relationships and daily experiences. They can create or shut down opportunities, build or destroy relationships, and uplift or discourage those around us. In the workplace, when leaders carefully choose their words, they can galvanize teams, crystallize complex concepts, and pave the way for innovation.

When you interact with your team, peers, or stakeholders, every word you use carries a certain weight. Words begin meaningful conversations, providing the foundation upon which collaborative relationships are built. They can steer negotiations in your favor, align diverging viewpoints, and serve as the platform for shared visions. In contrast, imprecise or poorly chosen words can muddy the waters of communication, leading to misunderstandings, stalled projects, eroded trust, and conflict.

Our brains, hardwired to seek clarity and meaning, use words to construct our understanding of the world around us. When you choose your words, you're doing more than just filling airtime; you're shaping the narrative, influencing perceptions, and creating a lasting impact. Language gives form to our thoughts, offering a framework that our mind uses to categorize, evaluate, and internalize experiences.

In many ways, words are the tools we use to paint our version of reality. Just as an artist selects each color and brushstroke deliberately, so too should we be mindful in our choice of words. In a work environment where details matter and the stakes are high, using language effectively can be your strongest asset. It's a skill worth honing because, despite being a small component of the communication puzzle, the words we choose have ripple effects on our careers and interpersonal relationships.

# How you say it

## Tone of voice

In effective communication, the "how" of what you say may often speak louder than the words themselves. The importance of nonverbal communication has been highlighted in earlier chapters, however, now the focus will be on how nuanced elements like the tone, volume, and speed of your voice can impact how your message is received, as well as what people may notice about your body language in meetings.

Building upon Mehrabian's 7-38-55 rule, 38% of communication is from vocal quality—your tone, volume, pitch, and speed. Your voice is like a fingerprint of your emotions and intent, giving away far more than you might realize. Think about how your tone, pitch, and pace can change drastically depending on your mood. When you're excited, for instance, your voice naturally elevates in pitch and quickens in pace—as though you can't get the words out fast enough. My daughter often speaks like this when she is excitedly telling me stories about her day, and it's as though the words are falling out of her mouth! It's often impossible to understand the story because all the words get jumbled together. I usually have to ask her to slow down and repeat what she said. Your pitch may be similarly high-pitched when you're speaking to a young child. But while the pitch might be high, your tone shifts and becomes warm and nurturing, and your speed slows down to ensure you're understood. These are instinctive adjustments we make based on the situation.

Now, consider professional settings like meetings. You have the opportunity to use your volume, pitch, and tone to be a signal of your confidence and authority. Speaking at a volume that is easily heard, with a calm voice, and medium rate of speech. Failing to project your voice can inadvertently signal a lack of confidence or commitment to your ideas. In contrast, when someone is upset or angry, their voice often takes on a specific quality—tightness or even sharpness—that's easily discernible to listeners.

When it comes to public speaking, presentations, or sharing your ideas in meetings, it's crucial to modulate your voice to keep your audience engaged. A monotone voice will lose them, but varying your pitch, volume, and pace can help emphasize your key points, hold attention where you want it, and keep the audience engaged.

So, you see, our voices serve as an involuntary emotional barometer. And once we become aware of this, we can be more intentional about what we're projecting. Whether it's excitement, seriousness, or compassion, make sure what you are saying aligns with how you are saying it.

# Body language

According to Mehrabian's rule, body language accounts for 55% of communication—so, it's fair to say that body language adds many layers of meaning to the words stated. They add context and give a window into the emotional world of the person you are speaking with. You should always be attentive to what your body language is conveying and observant (as explained in Chapter 4) to the body language of your team and other stakeholders.

First, let's discuss facial expressions. If you're naturally serious and observant, you might not realize that your focused expression may be read as aloof or even unfriendly. This is something I have had to personally manage myself. Years ago, I often heard, "I didn't think you were a very nice person. You always seemed so serious and distant. I thought you were unfriendly, until I got to know you." I spent a lot of time explaining to people that I was observant and shy, and it took me a minute to feel comfortable in large group settings. It was not lost on me that, as a small business owner, it wasn't exactly helpful to seen as "unfriendly!" So, even though I wasn't an unfriendly person, how others interpret your expressions and body language do matter. Perception is often reality in communication, and your facial expressions can be a deal-maker or deal-breaker in how you connect with people. In my case, I made the choice to consciously look like the friendly person that I actually am by being more mindfully present, feeling more relaxed, and smiling more both when I was and when I wasn't interacting with people. I also spend a little less time observing and have chosen to interact more; it's been a more helpful way to get to know people.

Now, consider your posture and gestures in different settings. In a meeting, for example, if you are sitting with your arms crossed, your colleague or employee might interpret this as defensive or disinterested. It's important to remember that you're not just a participant in these spaces; you're also a communicator, intentionally or not. The same goes for when you're presenting in meetings or to customers. While crossed arms or hands in pockets might feel natural, they could send the message that you're not open to other perspectives, or perhaps not fully engaged with your audience.

Nonverbal cues serve multiple functions, such as:

- Reinforcement: A warm smile, attentive posture, and engaging tone can strengthen the positive message you aim to convey.
- Interaction regulation: Nonverbal signals can guide the flow of a conversation. A nod can signify agreement, while raised eyebrows may indicate surprise or skepticism.
- Emotion translation: Body language and tone often provide an unspoken context, helping the listener to adapt their communication style in real-time based on emotional cues.

When you are speaking, being intentional with your nonverbal cues requires vigilance. Maintain an open posture to signify engagement and openness. Uncross your arms, relax your shoulders, and make eye contact. These gestures broadcast your mental openness, reinforcing your spoken words.

When someone is speaking to you, make eye contact. Be observant. Gauge what their body language, tone of voice, and facial expression might be really saying. Does it align with their words? If there's a discrepancy, it provides an opportunity for deeper understanding or clarification.

I hope you are beginning to understand how nonverbal cues serve as a critical amplifier of your spoken words, capable of enhancing or undermining the message you intend to convey. When you're the one talking, maintaining eye contact and an open posture can significantly augment the transparency and credibility of your message. If you're the one listening, be equally mindful. Pay attention to the speaker's body language and tone, as these cues often reveal subtext that words alone may not capture.

But the story your body tells can be complex and context dependent. Cultural norms and personal idiosyncrasies, such as an unintentionally stern facial expression (as in my case), can easily lead to misunderstandings. This makes it important to approach nonverbal cues as a guide rather than a definitive indicator in every case.

So, as you navigate the complexities of your own communication make body language an active part of your conversation—conscious, intentional, and aligned with your goals. Your nonverbal cues can either magnify your message or muddle it, making it crucial to harmonize the two for truly impactful exchanges.

When words, tone, and body language are in sync, they collectively weave an authentic narrative that resonates emotionally with your audience. This coherence not only clarifies your message but also paves the way for deeper, more meaningful interactions. By consistently demonstrating this level of communicative competence, you cement trust and set the stage for long-term success.

## COMMUNICATION STYLES

Our styles of communication are learned from childhood, adolescence, and into adulthood. We learn that when we speak or behave in a certain way, our needs are met. And, while these ways of communicating might have been safe and helpful ways as a child or teen to get what you needed from the adults in your life when you were young, they aren't necessarily the best ways to communicate and fulfill those needs as an adult. Our different communication styles not only shape the dynamics of workplace interactions but also directly impact team cohesion and productivity.

As you look through the following descriptions of communication styles that are particularly challenging, be honest with yourself and take note of how you might be engaging in some of these behaviors.

*Passive/Submissive*: This communication style is often exhibited by individuals who shy away from conflict and prioritize others' needs over their own. Their subdued voice and minimal eye contact may signal a lack of self-assurance, making it challenging for them to take decisive actions. They often opt to minimize their physical presence, as if attempting to take up as little space as possible.

*Passive-Aggressive*: At first glance, this style might seem non-confrontational. However, beneath the passive exterior lies simmering resentment. These individuals often resort to indirect ways of expressing their displeasure, such as sarcasm, unreliability, or even gossip. Their tone may be deceptively gentle, but their actions reveal a propensity for undermining and causing conflict.

*Aggressive*: The aggressive communicator bulldozes through conversations, often disregarding others' perspectives in favor of their own viewpoints. They tend to speak loudly, interrupt often, and employ exaggerated gestures that can feel intrusive to your personal space. This style can create a workplace atmosphere that many find intimidating and unwelcoming.

*Manipulative*: This communication style is particularly insidious, as it's characterized by individuals adept at maneuvering situations to their advantage. Rather than making direct requests, they subtly coerce others into fulfilling their wishes, often making them feel obligated to comply. This creates an imbalanced power dynamic that can lead to feelings of exploitation.

Do you or someone on your team take up a lot of space? Who does most of the talking? Who doesn't listen to others' opinions or ideas? Who is really quiet, doesn't say much, and is often ignored?

By becoming aware of the pitfalls of these styles and identifying how you and your team members might be engaging in challenging behaviors, you can choose to make changes that will ensure a psychologically safe environment for all.

## The gold standard

Assertive communication stands as the gold standard for effective interpersonal interactions, particularly in a team setting. This approach is built on the principle of articulating your thoughts and needs unambiguously, while simultaneously demonstrating respect for others. Assertiveness isn't just about what you say, it's also reflected in your nonverbal cues—maintained eye contact, purposeful body language, and balanced vocal pitch and volume. When you communicate assertively, you're willing to take responsibility for your decisions, ask for what you need directly, and gracefully handle the risk of rejection.

Moreover, assertive communicators excel not just in expressing themselves but also in listening effectively. They create an inclusive atmosphere by respecting personal boundaries, listening attentively, and responding constructively. This style fosters genuine connections with others and eliminates the need for manipulative or passive-aggressive behaviors. By knowing your limits and refusing to compromise them for the sake of others' demands, you command respect and promote a culture of openness and mutual regard.

So, can you see how adopting an assertive approach could elevate your interpersonal effectiveness and lead to more successful outcomes? What changes can you make to your current communication to implement this style?

## Active listening

Active listening is an invaluable component of meaningful communication, yet it's often an overlooked skill. When you're in conversation with someone, how well are you listening? Are you the kind of person who truly absorbs what's being said, empathizes, and then formulates an insightful response? Or do you find yourself already crafting your next statement, diverting your focus away from the speaker? Do you hang on to each word, or do you fill in the gaps with your own assumptions based on the subject or the person talking?

It's a common misconception that most of us are excellent listeners. In reality, many people are mentally fast-forwarding, focusing on their own thoughts, concerns, or even solutions. Some barely pay attention while scrolling through social media or answering emails while someone is talking to them. Not listening often leads to interruptions, misunderstandings, and a skewed perception of the conversation.

Listening, however, is not merely a passive activity; it's an intricate process influenced by factors such as your mindset, preconceptions, your current emotional state, and your propensity for daydreaming. Your ability to be an open and objective listener can be compromised if you're preoccupied, stressed, or emotionally drained. But when you're relaxed and centered—perhaps because you've just wrapped up a big project or simply having a great day—you're more likely to be open and receptive to an employee bringing you a new challenge to solve.

So, how do you upgrade from just "hearing" to "actively listening"? Focus your full attention on the speaker. Maintain eye contact and eliminate distractions—your phone, background activities, or even your own rambling thoughts. It's crucial to be mentally present in the moment. Take note of their words, the tone in their voice, and the body language accompanying it. Resist the urge to interject with your opinions or experiences and really listen.

Moreover, use conversational prompts and nonverbal cues to indicate your engagement. Simple affirmations like, "I see," or "Really!" as well as reactive facial expressions can validate the speaker and build trust. These subtle indicators not only confirm that you're tuned in but also that you care about what's being said.

Here's a quick summary of what active listeners do:

- They intentionally absorb the entire message being communicated.
- They maintain an undivided focus on the speaker.
- They use nonverbal cues such as nodding or verbal affirmations to show engagement.
- They listen to understand, not just reply.
- They respond in a way that furthers the conversation.

Becoming an exceptional listener isn't an overnight endeavor, but with conscious practice and self-awareness, you can master the art of active listening.

# SHOWING YOU CARE

As a listener, you're not just a passive receiver of information, you're an active participant, filtering the conversation through your own emotional and intellectual lens. To genuinely understand the speaker's message and emotions, ask probing, open-ended questions for clarity and deeper insight. It's not merely about hearing the words but grasping the underlying sentiment, the context, and the unspoken nuances. This empathic engagement not only enriches your comprehension but equips you to respond in a way that validates the speaker and advances the conversation.

Responding meaningfully will mirror the depth of your understanding and attentiveness. Your reply should be tailor-made to the speaker's needs—do they seek advice, validation, or merely a compassionate ear? Do not attempt to "fix the problem" if they are seeking a compassionate ear; it will show that you aren't really listening fully. If you aren't sure what they want, ask. And refrain from interrupting unless absolutely necessary, as doing so typically disrupts the conversational flow and could be perceived as disrespectful. If you're unsure how to respond, especially in emotionally charged or complex situations, honesty is your best policy. Make it clear that you're trying to understand and frame your response in a way that is open, honest, and respectful.

# HANDLING DIFFICULT CONVERSATIONS

*Everything that irritates us about others can lead us to an understanding of ourselves.*

CARL JUNG

Having difficult conversations is an unavoidable but important aspect of any leadership role. Whether you're delivering

constructive criticism, sharing unpleasant news, or addressing conflicts, the ability to communicate calmly during tense
moments is essential. Most people would rather avoid these
conversations, but that can escalate tensions and erode trust,
causing more harm than good in the long run. Developing
your ability to handle these situations skillfully is imperative.

Navigating these conversations can be made a bit easier if
you follow these steps:

1.  *Act promptly*: Timeliness matters. Waiting too long to
    address an issue can complicate things and heighten
    emotions. Once you recognize a problem or a pattern
    of behavior that requires intervention, act promptly.
    The hesitation to tackle the issue head-on can escalate
    it into something even more problematic.
2.  *Be prepared*: Having these discussions without prepa-
    ration is a recipe for misunderstanding and further
    conflict. While you shouldn't prepare a script—since
    it will come across as insincere—you can identify key
    points and objectives for the conversation and write
    them down. Equally important is anticipating the
    other person's reactions, especially if they're likely
    to be defensive or confrontational. If the person has
    their own challenges with communication and hos-
    tility, be sure to have another person at the meeting
    with you.
3.  *Choose the setting carefully*: Where and when the con-
    versation takes place can significantly affect its out-
    come. Opt for a neutral, private space and a moment
    when both parties can fully engage in the dialogue
    without distractions. Grabbing someone when they
    are buried in work and have a tight deadline or rep-
    rimanding them in a public setting are not the best
    approaches for a difficult conversation.
4.  *Set the right tone*: Begin the conversation on a positive
    note, to set the stage for a constructive discussion.
    Being accusatory will likely cause the other person

to become quickly defensive. Frame your points in a way that communicates your perspective without attacking theirs. For example, instead of saying, "I can't believe you did this!" an alternative might be, "This project deadline has come and gone several times and we don't seem to be making any progress. It is very disappointing. I'd like to hear your perspective."

5. *Active listening and encouraging dialogue*: When it's the other person's turn to speak, be fully present. Listen attentively to understand their perspective, rather than focusing on your next response. This form of active listening can yield valuable insights that might alter your viewpoint on the matter at hand. Further enrich the conversation by giving them the opportunity to elaborate on their perspective. Utilize open-ended questions like, "What circumstances caused this to happen?" to prompt a more comprehensive and meaningful discussion.

Although these conversations are challenging and can be uncomfortable, they are essential for resolving conflicts, enabling mutual understanding, and ultimately promoting a healthier work environment.

# GIVING AND RECEIVING FEEDBACK

When leaders provide feedback to your team members, it is a valuable opportunity to meaningfully communicate with them and utilize all the skills we have discussed in this chapter. Feedback plays a vital part in shaping how your employees perceive their roles, contributions, and pathways to improvement. So, failing to give them regular and consistent feedback creates a vacuum of uncertainty, leaving employees in the dark about how they are performing. This frequently leads to disengagement and decreased morale, as employees may feel disconnected from their roles and unsure about how their contributions align with organizational goals. If you are one of the two-thirds of managers who reportedly feel "uncomfortable" when communicating with your employees (as noted earlier in this chapter), please do the necessary work to strengthen this skill so you can better support the work of your team members.

In many organizations, they define "regular and consistent feedback" as their once or twice a year performance evaluation. But it shouldn't take 6 or 12 months for an employee to get feedback that could improve their performance. It is a missed opportunity. However, a 2017 Gallup report noted that as many as 26% of employees get feedback less than once per year![21] I even met a woman at a conference recently who remarked that she was resigning from a job she'd worked at for two years and had never received any feedback from her superiors! This is unacceptable.

In work environments marked by frequent changes and high expectations, the ability of managers to communicate thoughtful, continuous feedback is a necessity. This managerial competence goes beyond simply relaying information; it involves the delicate balance of affirmation and constructive criticism, designed to encourage growth and improvement. Conversely, poorly communicated or infrequent feedback can lead to disengagement, confusion, and plummeting morale. This makes it imperative for leaders to master the art of giving and receiving feedback as an integral part of their role.

Giving feedback must extend beyond merely pointing out what went wrong. Managers need to approach it as an ongoing conversation to encourage continuous improvement. This includes focusing on what the employee is doing well and offering practical, actionable advice for what could be better. When done effectively, this cultivates a sense of partnership and shared objectives between the manager and the employee.

One of the best ways to provide regular feedback is having weekly one-to-one meetings with each member of your team. These meetings create a reliable setting for timely feedback and goal setting. And the consistency ensures everyone's aligned and accountable, so there are no surprises down the line.

## Key elements of effective feedback

When providing feedback, it should be:

- Goal-oriented
- Actionable and constructive
- Clear and unambiguous
- Supported by examples
- Timely and ongoing
- Observational, rather than assumptive
- Balanced with positive reinforcement

Feedback isn't a one-way street; it's equally important for managers to be receptive to input from their team members. Openly receiving feedback fosters a culture of mutual respect and continuous learning. Leaders can gain valuable insights into team dynamics, potential obstacles, and even their own leadership style through this reciprocal process.

Being on the receiving end of feedback necessitates an open mindset. Both employees and managers should view feedback as a tool for performance enhancement rather than a personal attack. If the feedback is unclear, asking questions for clarity is advised. Nonverbal cues, like body language and tone, also play a role in how feedback is received and should be considered by both parties.

Once feedback has been exchanged, reflection is the next step. Evaluate the information received and create a concrete, yet flexible, action plan. This plan will guide you towards achieving your goals and improving performance.

Recognizing employees is a key component of creating an engaging culture at work. However, according to a 2022 Gallup/Workhuman report, 81% of leaders say recognition isn't a major strategic priority of their company.[22] Contrary to what these leaders may think, recognition is an essential tool for letting your employees know they matter, and their efforts are noticed and valued.

Recognition can take many forms:

- Highlighting someone's initiative in a team meeting
- Acknowledging the successful completion of a complex task
- Celebrating career milestones

These acts of recognition should be genuine and specific to show employees they are genuinely valued. When recognition is consistent and woven into the fabric of feedback, it serves as a morale booster and encourages a culture of excellence.

A balanced approach to feedback and recognition can turn your team into an engaged, accountable, and highly productive force. This is how you bring out the best in them.

# THE POWER OF STORYTELLING IN LEADERSHIP

Storytelling is a pivotal skill for leaders, as it transforms communication into an art that engages, motivates, and inspires. It can sway opinions, change mindsets, and encourage action. At its core, storytelling is about forging a human connection. Leaders who master storytelling can create emotional engagement with their team members, stakeholders, and audience. This emotional resonance is crucial in leadership as it fosters a sense of belonging and alignment with the organization's vision. Stories allow leaders to convey complex ideas and values in a relatable and memorable way, making them more impactful than mere facts or directives.

Stories also serve as a powerful medium for expressing an organization's vision and values. A well-told story can encapsulate the ethos of a company and what it stands for, making these abstract concepts tangible and relatable. This clarity helps in aligning team efforts towards a common goal, ensuring that everyone is on the same page. In times of change or crisis, stories become a stabilizing force that can reinforce the core values and guide the organization through turbulence.

Effective storytelling is a key tool in your toolbox of communication strategies. Consider asking yourself the following questions:

- How would a story make a difference here?
- How might a story persuade or motivate my audience?
- Would it clarify complex information or illustrate an important idea?

By presenting ideas through stories, leaders can overcome resistance and skepticism in a way that logical arguments alone cannot. Stories have the unique ability to bypass the analytical brain and speak directly to our emotions, making them a potent tool for influencing behavior and decision-making.

Now, if you are thinking to yourself, "I'm not a very good storyteller," you are not alone. Some people do seem like natural-born storytellers. However, luckily for the rest of us, these skills can be mastered.

Improving storytelling skills as a leader involves a combination of practice, observation, and understanding of the key elements that make stories compelling.

1. *Learn from master storytellers*: Observe how skilled storytellers construct their narratives, use language, and emotionally engage their audience. Listen carefully when others are presenting and observe how they include stories. By analyzing the techniques of proficient storytellers—be they speakers at TED talks, writers, or filmmakers—you can gain insights into the art of sharing compelling stories.

2. *Understand and connect with your audience*: It is essential to tailor your stories to your audience. Leaders must be skillful at understanding their audience's perspectives, needs, and interests, and modify their stories accordingly. This ensures that the story resonates with those who are listening.

3. *Incorporate personal experiences and authenticity*: Authenticity is key in storytelling. Leaders should use their own experiences to craft stories that are genuine and relatable. Personal anecdotes are powerful as they humanize the leader, making their messages more impactful and memorable.

# KEY ELEMENTS OF A COMPELLING STORY

These elements together help create a story that resonates deeply with your audience:

1. *Structured narrative arc*: Every compelling story is anchored in a well-defined timeline, marked by a beginning that sets the scene, a middle that escalates the narrative, and an end that brings closure. This structure helps in maintaining engagement and guiding the audience through the journey.

2. *Single character focus*: At the heart of every story is a protagonist whose journey the audience follows. While other characters may play significant roles, the experiences, decisions, and development of the main character primarily draws the audience's attention and empathy.

3. *Triggering event*: There is an event or incident that occurs that propels the protagonist into action. This incident is crucial as it initiates the momentum and sets the course of the story, sparking interest and anticipation.

4. *Confrontation with challenges*: The story focuses on the protagonist's challenges and hurdles. These conflicts introduce tension and drama, creating an

opportunity for character development. How the protagonist navigates these obstacles offers insights into their character and resilience, making the story engaging and revealing.

5.  *Crossroads and resolution*: As the story nears its conclusion, a pivotal turning point emerges, leading to a resolution. The protagonist's journey reaches its peak, and the central conflict is resolved.

The quality of the communication within an organization sets the tone for everything else. It influences teamwork, shapes culture, and impacts employee well-being. Without high quality communication, trust beaks down and teams crumble. Keep honing your skills so you and your team can work together better.

## APPLYING THE LEARNING

Based on what you've read in this chapter, ask yourself the following questions:

*   What have you learned?
*   What are your areas of growth?
*   How will you apply your learnings from this chapter?

And then go a little deeper. Please be very specific.

*   What two or three things are you going to start doing? _____
*   What two or three things are you going to stop doing? _____
*   What two or three things do you already do that you can build on? _____

## Self-Reflection Questions

1. How do my communication styles vary with different team members, and what impact does this have on our mutual understanding and collaboration?

2. How consistent am I in my communications and relationships with colleagues and clients? Do I follow through on promises and maintain steady, reliable interactions?

3. Are there aspects of my communication that I could improve to be more effective and clearer?

4. How conscious am I of my nonverbal cues (like body language, tone of voice, and facial expressions) during conversations and meetings? How might these cues be interpreted by others, and do they align with the message I intend to convey?

5. When I give feedback, how do I ensure that it is constructive, clear, and respectful?

6. How open am I to receiving feedback, and how do I typically respond to it? How can I be more receptive?

# 6

# Compassionate Command: Leading with Heart and Understanding

*Learning to stand in somebody else's shoes, to see through their eyes, that's how peace begins. And it's up to you to make that happen. Empathy is a quality of character that can change the world.*

BARACK OBAMA

On January 12, 2010, the heartbreaking news of the earthquakes destroying parts of Haiti filled the media. Watching the anguish unfold in Port-au-Prince, I felt a deep sense of the pain and trauma that people were experiencing. While aid was focused on the immediate physical health, safety, and security needs, what seemed lacking was the emotional support people needed to process the immense devastation caused by a 7.0 magnitude earthquake. I felt I had to help.

For the next seven months, I coordinated an international mental health relief effort with Project Medishare, a nonprofit organization partnered with the University of Miami School of Medicine that had already been providing supportive healthcare in Haiti for 16 years at the time of the earthquake. I sent licensed mental health professionals from the US each week to provide mental health support for adult and child patients at the field hospitals in Port-au-Prince. I went down to Haiti twice myself.

Fred Rogers, the iconic host of *Mister Rogers' Neighborhood*, often recounted a saying from his mother: "Look for the helpers. You will always find people who are helping." Those words have always resonated with me, especially during crises. I've always been a helper, hardwired to want to assist those in need. When I encounter stories of pain, trauma, or hardship, because I can instinctively sense other people's pain, my first response is often to wonder how I might help.

Have you ever found yourself deeply moved by a news story about a tragedy affecting complete strangers, feeling an urge to help? Or been so emotionally invested in a TV show that you cried alongside its characters? Perhaps you've even tearfully listened to a friend as they told you about the loss of a loved one? If you have, you've experienced empathy.

Empathy is the ability to understand and share another person's feelings. It asks us to be able to put ourselves in someone else's shoes and see the world from their perspective, through their eyes. We understand the other person's experience as if we were experiencing it without necessarily having had the experience ourselves.

Compassion, on the other hand, goes a step further. While empathy can be seen as a passive understanding of the individual's perspective or situation, compassion includes an active desire to help. It's understanding someone's emotions *and* wanting to take action to alleviate their distress.

At work, empathy helps leaders and team members recognize the emotions of others, which can be a powerful tool in managing relationships and ensuring psychological safety. Compassion encourages people to translate this empathic understanding into supportive actions, like finding solutions to reduce stress and burnout when a colleague is struggling.

When you lead with empathy, you're acknowledging the humanity of your team, respecting their experiences, and, in turn, creating a work environment where each of them can truly thrive. Your leadership becomes a meaningful, emotionally intelligent endeavor that positively impacts both your team and your organization. Empathy is a superpower that helps set the stage for better communication, conflict resolution, and a solid foundation of trust because it allows leaders and teams to understand each other's emotional and psychological states. It is the first crucial step towards taking compassionate action and is the essential emotional groundwork that makes genuine concern and assistance possible. For this reason, strengthening your empathy skills is the main focus of this chapter.

But what if you aren't sure whether you even have empathy or compassion? What if stories of other people's hardships, whether in the news, at work, or even in your personal life, leave you unfazed? What if you never find yourself wondering how your actions or words might impact someone else's emotional state? If this resonates with you, it's important to recognize that empathy isn't a "one-size-fits-all" attribute. Not everyone experiences or expresses it similarly, and that's okay. But if you're looking to become more empathic and compassionate, especially in a leadership role where understanding, relating to, and supporting others is crucial, acknowledging this as an area for growth is the first step.

## THE SCIENCE BEHIND EMPATHY

Empathy is a complex human capability that enables us to tune into the emotions or perspectives of others. It's a two-step process. First, we perceive how someone else is feeling; then, we process that information to respond in a way that is appropriate. This isn't just an abstract emotional process, it's hardwired into our brain's architecture. Specialized neural circuits in the brain activate when we register the emotional or physical pain of another person, offering us a neural-based understanding of what they're going through.

This neural activity isn't just an internal response; it manifests physically. Your body may actually feel the pain—specifically emotional pain—that the other person is experiencing. This is not mere imagination; it's a neurobiological process where your brain temporarily replicates the thoughts and feelings of the other person. As a result, you get a firsthand emotional understanding, allowing you to feel what it's like to walk in their shoes, even if it's just for a moment.

Empathy is both an emotional and a cognitive response. The brain's ability to process another's pain or discomfort is crucial for our survival. In evolutionary terms, this capability enhances our instinct to avoid danger and compels us to help others, strengthening social bonds that are essential for human communities.

However, it's essential to note that empathy isn't a constant state. Factors like stress or going through personal difficulties can diminish our empathic abilities temporarily. When you're preoccupied with your own challenges, it can be harder to fully connect with someone else's emotional state, which can affect how you respond to them.

So, while empathy is fundamentally a part of the human experience, various internal and external factors can modulate it. Understanding the neuroscience behind empathy gives us not only an appreciation for its complexity but also insights into why it might fluctuate under different circumstances.

As much as I love the science, it sometimes helps to drill things down to the simplest terms. I describe empathy in my training sessions as "Putting yourself in someone else's shoes," "seeing through their eyes," and "feeling their feelings." It helps you establish and build social connections. Some say empathy is having a bit of a moment—kids are even learning about it in schools; by learning empathy at a young age, children will develop the skills necessary to navigate diverse social situations with sensitivity and awareness.

Why, then, is empathy so important when it comes to growth, leadership, and career success? Because empathy helps you build better relationships, gives you a greater and deeper understanding of others, and allows you to move forward with more rational and well-informed decisions. Having strong connections is important for both mental and physical well-being and can help you go far in life. But it also helps you regulate your own emotions.

It's important to mention here that emotional intelligence, or EI, plays a significant role in our discussion about

COMPASSIONATE COMMAND 121

empathy. If you recall from our first chapter, higher EI is strongly linked to not only professional success but also to fulfilling relationships and overall well-being. Daniel Goleman, who popularized the concept of EI, identified empathy as an integral part of his emotional intelligence framework, specifically within the domain of social awareness empathy allows us to tune into others' emotional states, understand their needs, and respond appropriately.

Having the ability to understand how others are feeling goes deeper than just recognizing their emotions. You must then be able to use this information to adapt how you respond to them in a genuine way. If someone is grieving, for example, and you truly understand how devastated they must feel, you're more likely to treat them with the appropriate care they need to feel comforted and that their experience matters to you.

Being empathic can help guide the way you interact with all people—whether that's stakeholders and senior leaders or those just starting their career. And when you improve your ability to empathize, you can begin to interpret different situations or interactions in a more insightful way.

## TELL-TALE SIGNS OF AN EMPATHIC LEADER

*Leadership is about empathy. It is about having the ability to relate to and connect with people for the purpose of inspiring and empowering their lives.*

OPRAH WINFREY

In the past, empathy was considered to be an innate trait you either have or don't have, but more recent research shows that empathy is a skill—one that can be cultivated and refined with effort and focus.[23] While it's true that many people acquire a baseline level of empathy skills as they're growing up, even if you didn't, you can still develop them. Additionally, real-life challenges, whether experienced by you or someone close to you, serve as powerful drivers for developing empathy.

But parents and other adults do play a pivotal role in nurturing empathy during our childhood by both modeling care and concern and encouraging understanding and compassion. The importance of this initial influence can't be overstated. How parents attend to their children's emotional needs—especially in moments of fear or pain—sets the stage for empathy. Similarly, observing how adults demonstrate care and concern for each other, along with direct guidance on how to be considerate of playmates and siblings, further reinforces a child's ability to develop empathy.

Most of us have some degree of empathy already present, waiting to be honed and put to use. But, even if empathy was not a significant part of your early life lessons, it's a capacity that can be consciously developed at any stage of life. The crucial point is that it's never too late to invest time and energy into strengthening this invaluable skill.

A question that I frequently get asked is about the relationship between empathy and kindness in the workplace. The two are undeniably interconnected. Research supports this link, showing remarkable benefits for businesses that prioritize kindness and empathy. For instance, a 2018 study found that employees who experience kindness at work are 278% more generous with their co-workers compared to those in a control group.[24] But the impact doesn't stop there. Kindness also elevates overall well-being in the workplace, leading to increased energy, a more positive outlook, and enhanced problem-solving skills. The decision to integrate kindness, empathy, and compassion into your leadership style serves as a strategic business approach that lowers turnover, encourages innovation, and strengthens workforce resilience. It's a win-win-win for you, your team, and the organization.

Empathy stands as a foundational element for establishing trust and transparency. When you tune in to your employees' needs—be it the struggles they may be having with their workload, personal life challenges affecting their performance, or communication issues—you lay the groundwork for a relationship built on trust. The impact of empathic leadership is not just anecdotal; research indicates that 90% of US workers attribute higher job satisfaction to empathic leadership, while 79% believe it plays a significant role in reducing employee turnover.[25]

So, if your goal is to create a workplace where employees are satisfied and less likely to seek opportunities elsewhere, empathy is a must-have skill.

What are the signs of an empathic leader, then? You might be able to notice and label some of your own attributes, traits, or characteristics that could signal a high level of empathy.

Do any of the below sound like you?

- You have been told you're a good listener.
- You have the ability to "pick up" on how others are feeling, and act on it appropriately.
- You truly care about how people around you are feeling.
- People come to you with their problems or frequently ask you for advice.
- You have a "knack" for telling when people aren't being truly genuine.

In his book on emotional intelligence, Daniel Goleman identified five key elements of empathy:

1. Understanding others—sensing how others feel and taking an active interest in their concerns.
2. Developing others—acting on someone's needs and helping them to develop to their full potential.
3. Having a service orientation—Goleman described this using the example of those people who, in a work scenario, are seen as "going the extra mile" for others—because they genuinely care and want to help.
4. Leveraging diversity—creating opportunities through a diverse set of people and being aware and open to the fact that everyone has something to offer, no matter their age, gender, or race, for example.
5. Political awareness—in a work scenario, this refers to those who are aware of—and able to deal with—

office politics, for example. They'll be able to identify potential tensions and respond in a way that addresses people's concerns.

# EMPATHY FOR YOURSELF AND OTHERS

When we talk about empathy, we often focus on extending understanding and compassion towards others. However, one crucial facet that tends to be sidelined is self-empathy. It's vital to understand that empathy isn't a one-way street aimed solely at understanding others; it also involves being empathic towards yourself. When you're navigating life's challenges or dealing with setbacks, self-empathy enables you to treat yourself with kindness rather than succumbing to the harsh criticisms of your inner voice. Contrary to the notion that you should "just get over it," self-empathy helps you approach your own emotional world with the same understanding and care that you would extend to someone else. Failing to do so can lead to self-inflicted emotional distress.

Research supports the idea that continuously prioritizing others' emotional needs over your own can have drawbacks. Those who do so often find themselves experiencing feelings of low mood or even generalized anxiety. The root cause? Becoming too absorbed in others' emotional states, to the point where it influences your own emotional well-being. This absorption can lead to emotional fatigue and even create a sensation of being in the box of someone else's emotional life. While it's commendable to be so considerate of others' feelings, ignoring your own can be detrimental.

Empathy, then, is not just about understanding the emotional and cognitive complexities of others; it's also about maintaining a balanced perspective that includes your own needs and emotions. Self-awareness plays a pivotal role here. Being attuned to how deeply you're involving yourself in others' emotional states allows you to modulate your responses. It helps you find the right equilibrium between showing empathic concern for others and ensuring that your own emotional and psychological needs are not compromised. Remember, empathy is most effective when it's balanced, serving not just those around you but also enriching your own emotional intelligence and well-being.

# BUILDING YOUR EMPATHY SKILLS

Let's begin by debunking a common misconception: empathy is not an innate quality just reserved for a select few; rather, it's a skill that can be cultivated by anyone. So, everyone and anyone can build their empathy skills. Just like the other leadership skills, emotional intelligence, and communication techniques discussed in this book, empathy is an ongoing learning process. Whether you are a seasoned leader or a newbie in the professional world, there's always room to fine-tune your empathy skills. It's a journey rather than a destination (like most other things), and everyone starts from their unique point on the empathy continuum.

Importantly, it's worth noting that many individuals on the spectrum of autism do experience empathy, though many may not realize it. While some may struggle with conventional social cues, making their empathic responses less apparent, this often has more to do with social communication challenges than an absence of emotional response. In other words, their experience of empathy may not always manifest in ways that are commonly recognized, but that doesn't negate its existence. Awareness and understanding of these nuances can help not just those on the spectrum, but also those around them.

So, whether you're a naturally empathic person looking to deepen your skills, or someone who struggles with this form of emotional engagement—perhaps due to a neurodivergent condition like autism—you're not alone. The key takeaway is that empathy is a universally accessible skill, one that can be honed and developed, irrespective of your starting point.

Understanding what empathy is and how you experience it currently is essential. But the most crucial thing to ensuring empathy successfully emerges in your relationships is practicing it, building on it, and allowing it to grow in your life—which is why this next section may be the most important part of the chapter.

There are so many ways you can build your empathy muscle—take a look and see what resonates with you most.

## Ensure empathy starts with you

To strengthen your empathy muscles, you want to ensure you're being empathic with yourself, first. As mentioned previously, it is really important to tell your version of Negative Nelly or Critical Chris to please be quiet with the negativity and give them the job of becoming your favorite cheerleader.

Here is a helpful, brief exercise to practice being kinder to yourself:

Think of something you are struggling with right now. It could be work pressure, or a challenge in your personal relationships, or even difficulties you're having with your own personal growth. What are your thoughts on the situation? How do you feel about it? And what is your internal dialogue telling you in response to it?

Now, imagine a friend has come to you with the same problem. What would your perspective be then? How would you respond to them? It's likely there'll be a stark difference between the kindness you would show your close friend with the same problem and the lack of kindness you are giving yourself. In my experience, high performance individuals are often the worst at taking aim at themselves. They can struggle with vicious self-talk, ruminating on perceived flaws and criticizing their every misstep. Usually, people place much more blame and criticism on themselves than the kindness they'd offer up to their friend.

Practice treating yourself with kindness and giving yourself the empathic words, you would give your friend. Be forgiving and patient with yourself. Write down the impact of this exercise in a journal.

# Cultivate your curiosity

Curiosity serves as a starting point for empathy, providing you with an avenue to go more deeply into understanding others. It's all about asking questions that provoke deeper thought. Why is something the way it is? How did someone arrive at that conclusion? What implications does this have? Imagining scenarios like "What would it be like to be in their shoes?" or "What caused them to react the way they did?" helps you shift from surface-level understanding to a more nuanced view of the situation.

The power in this approach often lies in the questions themselves, not necessarily the answers you might get. When you ask meaningful questions, you're making a conscious effort to go beyond your initial thoughts and reactions. This doesn't mean you have to transform into a philosopher overnight; it simply calls for you to slow down and create room for reflection. By doing so, you're practicing a form of intellectual humility, acknowledging that your perspective is just one among many.

Try practicing curiosity at work with your colleagues by asking more questions:

1. "What led you to this point of view (or feeling)?"
2. "Can you help me understand your thought process?"
3. "What's important for you in this situation?"
4. "What challenges are you facing that I might not be aware of?"
5. "How would you like to be supported in this?"

Questions framed in this way encourage a deeper understanding of the other person's experience and perspective.

You can also practice on yourself by wondering:

1. "What assumptions am I making about this situation (or person)?"
2. "How might I feel and respond if I were in their position, taking into account their unique background, experiences, and perspectives (and not my own)?"
3. "What emotions am I experiencing right now, and why?"
4. "What biases might be influencing my perspective?"
5. "What do I not understand about this situation, and what can I do to gain a clearer perspective?"

Taking the time to ask yourself questions like these can help you pause and consider your own thoughts and feelings, as well as those of others.

## Tune in to the feelings of those beyond your inner circle

It's natural to feel more empathy towards those you're close to; you're already attuned to their emotions, which is likely one of the reasons they're in your inner circle to begin with. But what about everyone else—your colleagues, casual acquaintances, or even strangers? Expanding your empathic reach beyond what feels most comfortable can deepen your understanding of people more broadly.

To begin, consider those in your life whose feelings you may not often acknowledge. Take a day to mentally step into their world. If it's a colleague, ask yourself what job-related stresses they might be facing, or what personal pressures could be affecting them. Understanding things from their viewpoint not only broadens your perspective but can also change the way you interact with them.

However, imagining their feelings is just the starting point. To truly understand them, it's valuable to engage in conversation. This adds a layer of depth to your empathic skills, taking them from theoretical to practical.

# Engage in a disagreement

I know this one may sound a little bit odd. And it may not begin as the most comfortable of conversations, but these are often the types of interactions that are either badly handled or completely avoided, and we need to practice handling them better.

Engage in a conversation with someone who has a significantly different viewpoint to yours, someone you really disagree with. But in this instance have the conversation without it turning into a debate where you're forcing your opinion and disregarding theirs.

Instead, begin the conversation having an open mind and choosing to really listen to their point of view. Keep the idea of "listening to understand" at the forefront of your mind. I'm not suggesting you have to agree with the other person by the end of the conversation. What I am saying, however, is that if you genuinely listen to their perspective and how they formed it, you'll be well on your way to having a respectful, meaningful discussion that deepens your understanding of differing viewpoints.

# Become an active listener

Active listening is a topic we've touched upon many times before in this book, and for good reason. Its role in multiple facets of our life, particularly in nurturing empathy and forming connections with others, is critically important. Here's a startling statistic that highlights this: while a whopping 96% of global professionals believe they're good listeners, research shows that we actually absorb only about 50% of what's being said to us.[26] That's right, half!

Why such a big gap? The usual suspects are our own internal mind chatter and emotional distractions, rehearsing our own responses, and yes, even pondering what's for dinner. These mental diversions can severely hamper our ability to truly empathize, leading to misinterpretations and misunderstandings. It doesn't help that the normal adult rate of speech is between 100–150 words per minute, but our brain can process words at a rate of 400–800 words per minute, leaving us so much extra time for daydreaming.[27]

So, if we want to develop real empathy, we need to be all in when we're listening. This means keeping your focus razor-sharp, actively engaging with what the other person is saying, and resisting the temptation to let your mind wander. By tuning in completely, you're not just hearing—you're understanding, which is the cornerstone of empathy.

## Read widely

Many people easily lose themselves in books, while others struggle to maintain this habit. I have always loved reading and used to devour fictional novels, sometimes reading multiple books weekly. Books told me stories about people, their lives, their feelings, and how they dealt with difficult life circumstances and complex emotions. I was always more interested in the dialogue, the descriptions of the characters, and how they felt than I was in the descriptions of the imagery or the furniture. I spend much less time reading fiction these days, but I always keep a library of fiction novels at hand, so I am ready to read recreationally when I have some relaxing downtime.

Fictional stories offer us a unique gateway into the minds of characters, letting us experience their thoughts and emotions firsthand—people of different ages, genders, race, cultures, abilities, and life experiences. Since the characters often live lives vastly different from our own, we gain exposure to situations and challenges we might otherwise never encounter. But, whether it's fiction or nonfiction, hardback, paperback, Kindle, or audiobook, books give us insights into the worlds of other people, and this broadens our understanding of and empathy for people.

# Step outside your comfort zone

Challenging yourself to step outside your comfort zone is a powerful method for developing empathy. At work, you might tackle a challenging project that stretches your skills, or perhaps you'll decide to learn something entirely new—a skill you've shied away from or told yourself you're not capable of mastering. Don't limit yourself to the office, though. In your personal life, you might try volunteering in a community you're unfamiliar with or taking a class in a subject that's always intrigued you but seemed too intimidating.

Why do this? Venturing into unknown territory brings us a level of humility. It reminds you that you're not an expert in everything, and that's perfectly okay. It makes you more receptive to the experiences and wisdom of others. Whether it's grabbing coffee with a work colleague you've only exchanged passing hellos with, or joining a community organization as a newbie, these experiences help you see the world through different lenses, enriching your own perspective and deepening your understanding of others.

# Identify your biases

Identifying, understanding, and shifting your biases are a recurring topic in this book for good reason: they play an enormous role in both your personal and professional interactions. When biases cloud your judgment, your ability to empathize suffers dramatically.

These biases, whether they are based on race, ethnicity, age, social standing, or anything else, act like filters that distort how you receive and interpret information from others. They establish barriers that obstruct you from truly understanding someone else's perspective and emotions—essentially blocking the core function of empathy.

The journey to dismantle these biases begins with acknowledgment. Ask yourself, what negative stereotypes are you holding onto? Why do they exist in your mindset? What's their origin? It's an uncomfortable but necessary process.

Once you've identified these biases, the next step is to challenge them. Reflect on what experiences you may or may not have had with a specific group you may have biases against. If you find you have limited or no experiences with a particular group, consider it an opportunity to learn and broaden your understanding. Actively seek out information, stories, or even friendships that can challenge your preconceived notions. It's also crucial to recognize that each person brings their own unique experiences and perspectives to the table, rather than categorizing everyone as part of a single, monolithic group.

Look for what you share in common with individuals rather than focusing on the differences. By seeking out these similarities, you create the conditions for better interpersonal interactions.

## Be vulnerable

While many empathy-building strategies involve focusing on and interacting with others, we must also turn the lens inward towards ourselves. Vulnerability plays a crucial role here. By deeply engaging with our own emotions and being open about them with ourselves and others, we create the space for empathy to flourish. Not only does vulnerability help us better understand our own feelings, but it also enhances our ability to recognize and interpret emotions in others.

In the workplace, vulnerability often manifests as a willingness to admit when you're wrong, a readiness to share credit for successes, and an openness about your own feelings and uncertainties. For leaders, building vulnerability might involve stepping away from the traditional idea of you having all the answers. Instead, you might begin team meetings with candid discussions about project challenges, inviting input from everyone. It could also mean taking the time to listen to team members, not just about their work but about their personal highs and lows. By modeling this behavior, leaders not only encourage a culture of trust and openness, but they also make it easier for others to share, collaborate, and feel emotionally invested in their work.

It takes courage to be vulnerable—it's absolutely not a sign of weakness (as you may believe). Embracing vulnerability makes you authentically you, and that authenticity encourages trust among the people around you. Without the ability to be vulnerable, we lack the emotional open channels that are essential for empathy.

As we've explored the many aspects of empathy, I hope the overarching message is clear: leaders who practice empathy don't just understand the people they lead, they also guide the way for a culture where everyone feels valued, understood, and motivated. Take these insights and strategies to heart, incorporate them into your leadership toolbox, and watch as they not only enrich your interpersonal relationships but also positively influence your team's success.

## APPLYING THE LEARNING

Based on what you've read in this chapter, ask yourself the following questions:

- What have you learned?
- What are your areas of growth?
- How will you apply your learnings from this chapter?

And then go a little deeper. Please be very specific.

- What two or three things are you going to start doing? _____
- What two or three things are you going to stop doing? _____
- What two or three things do you already do that you can build on? _____

## Self-Reflection Questions

1. Can I recall a recent instance where I genuinely understood and shared the feelings of a colleague, and how did that empathy influence our interaction?
2. In what ways has my capacity for empathy influenced my decision-making processes?
3. Can I recall a specific instance where considering others' feelings or situations led to a more inclusive or effective decision?
4. How do I usually deliver difficult feedback to an employee? How might I adapt my approach next using more empathy?

# PART 3

# Cultivating the Whole Leader: Embracing Personal Renewal and Collective Strength

# 7

# Sustained Growth: Renew, Recharge, and Refuel for the Journey Ahead

*If you feel burnout setting in, if you feel demoralized and exhausted, it is best, for the sake of everyone, to withdraw and restore yourself.*

DALAI LAMA

In much of corporate, business, and organizational culture, the emphasis has often been on relentless ambition, tenacity, and an unyielding drive to succeed. Historically, leaders have frequently set their own needs aside, pushing forward through challenges with the belief that self-sacrifice is an inherent part of their role.

However, there's no escaping the adage "You cannot pour from an empty cup."

The reality is leaders are not immune to the psychological and physical tolls of constant stress and demands. I can't tell you how many of my clients struggle with integrating their well-being with the demands of their work. They tell themselves that it is required of their role and that they are just "being more productive."

However, they are so very wrong. Sustained growth requires periods of renewal, recharging, and refueling. Self-care drives well-being. People are significantly *more* productive when they're well rested, fueled well with good nutrition, and energized from moving their body.

Self-care is fundamentally about taking steps to maintain and improve your physical, emotional, and mental well-being. It starts with listening to your body and mind and making thoughtful choices. This can range from looking at your diet, sleep patterns, and exercise routines, to engaging in activities like creativity, mindfulness, and gratitude exercises. It's not just a one-time activity; it's an ongoing commitment to positively support your well-being.

Consistent self-care practices have been scientifically validated to diminish symptoms of anxiety and depression, lower stress levels, enhance focus, alleviate feelings of frustration and anger, elevate mood, and boost energy. A dedicated self-care regimen has been shown to improve physical health and mitigate the risk of stroke, heart disease, and cancer.

Setting boundaries is a key component of self-care, serving as a proactive measure to avoid overwhelm and burnout. When your plate is already full and you find yourself juggling too much, understanding when to say "no" or decline additional commitments becomes crucial. Whether it's declining a social event to have some alone time, or making sure you leave work on time a few days a week, setting these boundaries contributes to a healthier, more balanced life.

A common misconception is that self-care is selfish, when actually the opposite is true. Taking care of yourself puts you in a better position to be present for others. Your relationships improve, and you find that you have more patience and empathy to offer. In short, self-care empowers you to be a better friend, family member, and colleague.

Self-care is personal and flexible; it doesn't have a fixed look or format. It varies from person to person and can even change for you over time based on your evolving needs. Many people make the mistake of only focusing on self-care when they're already burnt out. The key is to make it a consistent part of your life. It's not about spending money on lavish experiences; it's about identifying the small, everyday actions that bring you peace and make you feel good.

Repeat after me: *self-care is not selfish.*

# SELF-CARE FOR HOLISTIC LEADERSHIP

Just as a well-maintained machine operates at peak efficiency, leaders who prioritize their well-being set the stage for longevity, clearer decision-making, and better communication leading to working better with their teams. It is essential for leaders to recognize the critical importance of self-care to keep themselves and their teams growing.

If you're picturing self-care as just some new-age hippy trend, let's set the record straight. The buzz around self-care in today's culture has painted a glitzy picture, often filled with images of opulent wellness retreats or tied to trendy hashtags showcasing cute highlight reels. But these mainstream depictions, as prevalent as they might be, can sometimes minimize what self-care truly embodies. Beyond the glitz and glamour lies the fundamental essence of self-care, rooted in personal introspection and genuine attention to one's needs.

Now don't get me wrong, if you want to go to a spa or retreat, I am quite certain you will find it both relaxing and energizing. However, don't think of self-care as a fleeting trend or reserved only for specific groups or at special times. It's necessary for everyone. And it isn't only about meditation and mindfulness. At its heart, self-care is about intentionally pausing, reflecting, and genuinely tending to one's needs, whatever they may be, *daily*.

Ask yourself:

- What activities instill a sense of well-being and contentment within you?
- How well are you taking care of your physical, mental, and emotional needs?
- What steps can you take to improve your physical health?
- What are you doing to connect with others?
- What calms the incessant chatter of your mind and shuts out the noise?
- What brings you a sense of peace, calm, and tranquility?

Your answers to these questions will shape your personal self-care routine.

Since we each have our own unique set of preferences and sources of peace and calm—for some, like me, self-care might look like long walks with my dog along the river, vigorous workouts and boxing at the gym (yes, this helps me relax), or a deep breathing session at the end of a long day to settle my mind. For others, self-care might be the simplicity of remembering to take a shower and eat breakfast every morning or making time to socialize with friends. Yours will be unique to you. It's the individuality of these practices that makes them truly enriching.

# MANAGING YOUR ENERGY

When we talk about energy, it's not just about physical stamina or electrical power. Humans are made up of energy—right down to our cells and atoms. Our emotions, thoughts, and even the chemical and electrical reactions in our bodies are forms of energy. Think of it like a battery. When your battery is fully charged, you're more in sync with yourself and the world around you. You're not just physically awake—you're also more emotionally and mentally engaged. Conversely, when that battery runs low, you'll struggle to focus, connect with others, or even muster the enthusiasm to face the day.

In the workplace, energy is more than a personal trait—it's a collective currency that connects us, can make or break team dynamics, influence mental health, and even steer the company culture. It's something we all bring with us, whether stepping into a meeting room or sitting down to tackle a challenging project. Our energy manifests in myriad ways: the tone of our voice, our posture, and even the expressions that cross our face. It sets the stage for everything that follows, from communication and collaboration to the ultimate success or failure of a project, because they depend on the energy we bring each day.

Simon Alexander Ong beautifully articulates this contagious nature of energy in his book *Energize*.[28] He points out that energy, whether positive or negative, can spread like wild-fire. It can inspire your colleagues, creating a ripple effect of enthusiasm and productivity, or it can engulf the team in a tidal wave of negativity and chaos. As leaders, this places a tremendous responsibility on our shoulders. Our energy doesn't just impact us; it shapes our interactions, team functioning, and the entire organization's culture.

Now, think about how closely this concept of energy is tied to well-being, particularly in high-stress environments vulnerable to burnout. When your energy is depleted, it shows across all facets of your being—your emotional balance, your cognitive abilities, and your interpersonal relationships. A leader running on low energy risks eroding essential elements that make a workplace both productive and humane, such as psychological safety, trust, and inclusivity.

Therefore, understanding and managing your energy is not an act of self-care just for you; it's an act of communal care. When your "fuel tank" is full, you're not only more productive and less prone to the effects of stress, but you also contribute positively to the work environment. This becomes a kind of virtuous cycle. A fully charged leader sets the tone for their team, encouraging an atmosphere where everyone feels emotionally supported and intellectually stimulated.

# THE CRUCIAL LINK BETWEEN SELF-CARE AND BURNOUT

The World Health Organization characterizes burnout as a syndrome arising from unmanaged, chronic workplace stress, marked by exhaustion, cynicism about work, and reduced effectiveness.[29] In the US, 77% of professionals report experiencing burnout, with over half saying it's happened more than once.[30] Similarly, a 2022 study by Spring Health found that 76% of US workers felt burnout in the past year.[31] The kicker? Both studies point to poor self-care as a significant factor that can exacerbate or prolong burnout.

The Spring Health researchers specifically highlighted that consistent self-care is one of the most effective ways to avoid and mitigate burnout, yet many people only start to focus on self-care when they've already hit their limit.

This reality is puzzling considering that everyone agrees that self-care has tangible benefits for both your physical and mental health, including reduced stress and improved relationships. According to a 2020 Harris Poll survey for Samueli Integrative Health Programs, 80% of US adults expressed a desire to focus more on self-care post-pandemic.[32] But when we fast-forward to 2023, the statistics paint a different picture: only about 36% are actually making self-care a daily priority, a concerning disconnect given its proven advantages.[33]

Usually, when the topic of self-care comes up with my clients, it's often in the context of burnout... as in they're exhausted, not sleeping well, without physical activity, not eating properly, and sitting at a desk all day long, and then they are wondering why both physically and emotionally they are feeling poorly. Some get so focused they even forget to shower or eat. These are the conversations I have been having with clients for literally decades. I remember getting a new client many years ago for therapy, a lawyer, because she ended up in the hospital emergency room and then into the ICU because her body was shutting down. The cause? Burnout and stress. The prescription: self-care and therapy. I find one consistent pattern across many of my clients: people are often resistant to taking the time to care for themselves.

I remember years ago watching one of Oprah Winfrey's television programs and she said,

> *Difficulties come when you don't pay attention to life's whisper. Life always whispers to you first, but if you ignore the whisper, sooner or later you'll get a scream.*

I have never forgotten her statement and I explain this to many of my clients all the time. Your mind and body give you hints. Hints that you are not taking proper care of yourself, and your fuel tank is starting to empty. These are the whispers. If you ignore them and keep pushing, forcing yourself to struggle through with low energy, poor sleep, and no fuel, your body and mind will rebel. And the whispers will keep getting louder and louder until, one day, you end up really unwell for some reason and forced to stop and take the time needed to recover and get well. Please don't wait until you end up in the hospital or with serious health problems.

## MY RECOMMENDATION: PAY ATTENTION BEFORE IT GETS TO A SCREAM!

In an ideal world, we'd prioritize self-care before we reach this point, by paying attention to the warning signs of burnout in order to prevent it. Warning signs may be feeling negative consistently about your work, feeling like your workload is never ending and is taking over your life, working much longer hours, not eating properly, struggling to sleep, and beginning to feel a sense of doom. Take the time to make yourself a priority.

Learning how to add self-care rituals into your life is an important step.

## WHAT ARE YOUR STRESS TRIGGERS?

Stress is your body's immediate reaction to any kind of pressure that prompts a need to survive. It could also be a perceived threat, challenge, or scare. This could be, for example, having a job interview, preparing for a big presentation, or having too many job responsibilities or tasks on your to-do list. If this just happens once or once in a while, it isn't much of a problem. However, when stressors pile up one on top of another and another and another, without any relief, there's a problem.

"Stressors" are events or conditions in your surroundings that may trigger stress. Your body responds to stressors differently depending on whether the stressor is new or short-term—which we'd call acute stress—or the stressor has been around for a longer time—which we'd define as chronic stress.

These can be broken down further into internal or external stressors. External stressors are events and situations that happen to you, caused by something external to you. In the workplace, common external stressors include an impossible workload, endless emails, urgent deadlines, or a demanding boss. Most people experience work-related stress in the form of tension or anxiety at least occasionally, regardless of their industry or career. However, others experience almost nonstop stress due to intense working conditions.

Internal stressors, on the other hand, are the thoughts that pop into your head and cause you distress. These stressors can include the voice of your inner critic, fear—such as a fear of failure, thoughts of uncertainty because of a lack of control of your situation, or even a feeling of apprehension over the expectations of your role at work.

It's important to be aware of what may be causing your stress reactions, so you can work to manage it in an appropriate way. Once you have acknowledged it, you can begin to work on finding tools and techniques to refuel and recharge or shift the way you are thinking about the situation using the Thoughts>Feelings>Actions>Results tool in Chapter 1.

## THE "I DON'T HAVE TIME" CONUNDRUM

The excuse of "not having time" for self-care is one I hear often, especially from those who are perpetually busy. Their jam-packed schedules make them feel as though they can't afford to slow down, even when slowing down is exactly what they need. This creates a vicious cycle—being "too busy" to invest in self-care doesn't stop the work and the extra commitments—you will eventually burnout. The irony here is that many of these people have adapted to a lifestyle of constant activity to the point where being overworked feels normal. Adding self-care to this equation might seem overwhelming, but it's important to realize that self-care doesn't require a huge time commitment. Integrating it into your daily routine can actually make you feel less stressed and improve your focus (and improving your focus will make you more productive but less busy).

Making time for self-care is really non-negotiable. Consider it an investment in your mental health and well-being, one that becomes easier to maintain once it becomes habitual. Think about it in the context of your daily walk or watching a favorite TV show—once it's a part of your routine, it doesn't feel like an added burden. Let's face it, life comes with its fair share of demands competing for our attention. Neglecting self-care is something we're all prone to do. However, the reality is that regular and consistent self-care improves your resilience and ability to handle life's curveballs. So, the next time you think you don't have time for self-care, remember that you can't afford *not* to make the time.

Bottom line: Make the time.

# THE BASICS

## Eat a healthy diet

The first place to start when we are discussing self-care is our diet. It's easy to assume that self-care only encompasses mental exercises or downtime, but what you eat significantly influences your well-being. Food is more than just fuel—it's an integral part of your overall health, impacting your mood, focus, and even your stress levels. Eating a balanced diet is not just about restraining yourself from over-indulgence; it's about enriching your body with the nutrients it needs to function optimally.

The relationship between food and well-being is reciprocal. A diet high in processed foods or sugars can not only affect your physical health but also contribute to feelings of fatigue, irritability, and even symptoms of depression. Conversely, consuming a balanced diet rich in nutrients can enhance your energy levels and sharpen your focus. And let's not forget the psychological benefits; knowing you're taking good care of your body can significantly uplift your mental state. So, the next time you consider what self-care means to you, don't forget to include healthy eating as a cornerstone of your overall strategy. Your reward will be a better sense of well-being, not just for the moment, but as a sustained lifestyle.

## Exercise

Exercise consistently appears on every self-care checklist, and there's a good reason for that—it's not just about physical health but mental well-being as well. The health benefits of regular exercise are backed by a plethora of scientific studies. According to the Centers for Disease Control and Prevention (CDC), physical activity doesn't just keep your body in shape; it's also an effective strategy for improving mental health.[34] The positive impact extends from enhancing cognitive functions to alleviating symptoms of anxiety and depression. It even uplifts self-esteem, making you more resilient to life's challenges.

However, the key to sustaining an exercise routine is to engage in activities that you genuinely enjoy. Too often, people gravitate towards workouts they think they "should" be doing, rather than those they enjoy. The result? A program that feels like a chore, rather than an empowering act of self-care. You don't have to run if you dread it, nor do you need to swim laps if the pool isn't your sanctuary. The array of options is vast—whether it's a calming walk in the park, a spirited dance class, a competitive tennis match, or a scenic cycling route. The most effective exercise for self-care is the one that you'll stick with because you love it, not just because it's good for you.

## Sleep

"I'll sleep when I'm dead." Not quite. Don't underestimate the power of sleep and how your body recharges and regenerates during those precious hours in the land of nod.

Current research suggests that the average adult requires at least seven hours of sleep per night.[35] If you're a night owl, you might find it harder to set yourself a bedtime each night, but giving yourself a specific time so you have at least the seven hours needed is a great way to ensure you get the right amount of sleep. If you have insomnia due to stress or hormonal problems, having a calming bedtime routine can be helpful. Deep breathing, soft calming music, or meditation often help. Giving yourself at least 30 minutes before bedtime is also suggested to reduce all blue light exposure (from screens and devices) and do another relaxing activity. I like to do deep breathing before I go to sleep. It settles my mind and almost always sends me to sleep pretty quickly.

## Practice gratitude

One of my daily self-care practices is the simple act of practicing gratitude. It has been especially effective for refocusing the mind on positive aspects of your daily life. Doing this can reshape your outlook and counter the constant stream of stressful or negative thoughts that frequently flood your mind and dampen your mood. I've found that the best time for me to practice gratitude is right before I go to sleep. It's the final thoughts my mind focuses on, helping me to end the day on a relaxing and positive note.

This is what I call a "micro-dose" of self-care, ideal for those moments when time is scarce, but you need a mental lift. Ask yourself, what are three things from today that made me feel good, brought a smile to my face, and that I'm genuinely grateful for? The answers could range from life's fundamentals—a roof over your head or your family's well-being—to something more specific, like a helpful colleague or the flexibility of working from home. Consistently listing these things, whether in the morning or, as I prefer, at night, can subtly but powerfully shift your perspective over time.

# Create your self-care toolkit

Creating a self-care toolkit is a practical strategy I've success-fully implemented with clients and for myself. I think of it as a go-to idea book of activities and practices that bring joy, peace, or a much-needed fun break when feeling mentally taxed. It's something you'll continually reference and add on to, and what's beautiful about it is that it's uniquely tailored to you, offering a range of activities that can fit into multiple areas of your life.

To build your toolkit, start by brainstorming activities that uplift you. These could be simple pleasures like making your favorite coffee at home, or something more involved like going for a long run in the sun. It might help to catego-rize these activities into those that are quick and easy, and those that require a bit more time or investment. The aim is to have a diverse set of tools at your disposal, giving you the flexibility to engage in self-care regardless of how much time you have.

Feel free to document this toolkit anywhere convenient, whether that's in a dedicated notebook or on the Notes app on your phone. Over time, these activities will become sec-ond nature, practically etched in your memory. And remem-ber, your toolkit is a living document; it's okay to adjust it as you go along, adding or removing activities based on your current needs and preferences.

If you're struggling to come up with ideas, consider some of these suggestions: a short walk to clear your mind, creating a calming playlist, running a warm bath for yourself, doing a 10-minute yoga YouTube video, curling up on the sofa under a blanket with your favorite book, or even calling a friend who always knows how to make you smile. The objective is to have a selection of options that you can pick from based on your mood and circumstance.

So, spend some time putting together your self-care tool-kit. It's a personal project focused solely on your well-being, so don't hesitate to fill it with activities that resonate with you. With this toolkit in hand, you'll have a structured way to engage in self-care, ensuring that it becomes a regular part of your life rather than an afterthought.

# MORE OPTIONS FOR PRACTICING SELF-CARE

In every chapter of this book, my goal has been to offer practical advice for improving your self-leadership across various areas of your life. When it comes to self-care, remember that it's an incredibly individualized concept. There's no one-size-fits-all approach. Aside from the important basics: eating healthy, exercising, getting enough sleep, and practicing gratitude, what's essential is grasping what self-care means to you personally. Once you discard preconceived notions—like equating self-care solely with meditation—you can find a meaningful way that resonates with you and start building it into your daily or weekly routine.

Starting small is often the most sustainable way to introduce self-care into your busy schedule. Forget about elaborate spa days or week-long wellness retreats for a moment. Focus on "micro" acts of self-care that you can easily integrate into your day. Whether it's a one-minute morning meditation, a quick power walk during lunch, or simply savoring a cup of tea away from your work, these small activities can serve as quick but effective ways to uplift yourself, especially when time is tight.

While these micro-doses of self-care are beneficial, let's not forget the importance of dedicating larger blocks of time to self-care to build a solid foundation. Depending on your personal and professional commitments, you might earmark an hour a week as "me time," where you engage in activities that rejuvenate you. Over time, you'll begin to notice the ripple effect this dedicated time has on your overall well-being. Whether you're juggling a busy career and/or caring for children or parents, making self-care a priority in your schedule will pay off significantly.

## Embrace humor

Kids laugh at just about anything. They laugh at a muddy puddle being splashed up their legs, they laugh at silly faces, funny noises, exaggerated dancing, loud singing. They're so present in the moment, they see the funny side of things a lot. One way we can really renew, recharge, and refuel for the journey ahead is to embrace laughter, embrace humor, and be more like a kid. And by that, I mean laugh when things are funny, watch a funny movie, and enjoy the humorous side of life. Sometimes it helps to not take things so seriously (something I keep having to remind myself). Don't be afraid to let go and release the need to be so serious all the time.

## Try out new things

If self-care feels like foreign territory, the road to discovering what truly nurtures you may require some experimentation. Think of it like sampling from a fabulous buffet of well-being. Each activity or practice you try serves as a "taste test" to gauge how it fits your personality and into your personal self-care routine. And remember, the goal is rejuvenation, not obligation. If an activity feels like another item on your to-do list, then it's probably not the right fit for your self-care toolkit. Instead, you should aim for practices that bring you a sense of peace, or perhaps even joy, both during the experience and in its aftermath.

Don't hesitate to look around and gather inspiration from people in your circles. Maybe a colleague raves about the tranquility they feel from early-morning yoga classes, or a friend finds peace in painting watercolors over the weekend. If it intrigues you, give it a whirl. You never know—you might discover a fulfilling self-care practice you hadn't considered. Keep an open mind—what works wonders for someone else might also do the same for you.

# Ask for help from others

There's an enduring myth that "being strong" means going it alone and shouldering all your burdens in silence. Let's debunk that right now: asking for help is not just acceptable, it's essential. Whether it's confiding in friends and family, seeking advice from colleagues, or talking things through with your boss, coach, or therapist, external support can be a transformative part of your self-care journey. It's not just about unburdening yourself, but also about gaining new perspectives, coping strategies, and perhaps even solutions that you hadn't considered.

We'll delve deeper into the intricacies of your support network in Chapter 8. You'll see how these interpersonal relationships play a pivotal role in your well-being and personal growth. A supportive community can be like a safety net, catching you when you're close to your tipping point, and helping you bounce back stronger. In the end, self-care doesn't mean isolating yourself; it means knowing when to reach out to fortify your own resilience.

# Analyze and reassess with a self-reflection tool

The best part of adding self-care into your daily lives, is to change it up when you need to. By that, I mean knowing when it's working and when it's not. Put a note in your calendar to reflect on your progress and how these practices are truly making you feel. If an act of self-care feels like a chore, it won't be giving you the balance and calmness you need. If you feel like there's something else that might give you that, swap it in.

# Wait, there's more!

- Read a book
- Write your thoughts down in a journal
- Go for a walk
- Listen to your favorite song

- Cook your favorite dinner
- Have a few hours away from your phone
- Prayer or spiritual time
- Get some sunshine on your face
- Enjoy a nap
- Spend time with people you love
- Give yourself a shoulder massage
- Come off social media for a day
- Watch some comedy
- Spend time in nature
- Draw, paint, or create
- Look through an old photo album
- Do a five-minute relaxation on YouTube
- Sing out loud
- Have a bath
- Practice yoga
- Take in five long, slow deep breaths
- Declutter one of your rooms
- Write down 10 things that bring you joy
- Do some morning stretches
- Light a scented candle and enjoy the smell
- Do something kind for someone else
- Go out to your favorite coffee shop for a coffee break
- Plan some social activities
- Watch the sunset
- Write a list of all your worries to get them out of your head
- Avoid screen time

Can you think of others?

# HOW TO MAINTAIN A SELF-CARE ROUTINE

Establishing a consistent self-care routine is often more challenging than conceptualizing one. We all have moments of inspiration—perhaps at the start of a new year or a new season—where we vow to transform our habits. Yet, these plans often fizzle out within weeks. The pitfalls are common:

either we set overly ambitious goals, select activities we don't genuinely enjoy, or lack accountability. To make your self-care routine stick, it's crucial to start with small, meaningful actions you believe in and share your intentions with someone close to make you accountable.

A sustainable self-care regimen can indeed work wonders for your mindset, relationships, and problem-solving abilities. But let's be realistic: it's not a one-size-fits-all solution. If you're consistently maintaining your routine but still find emotional or psychological challenges persist, or the stress seems overwhelming, don't hesitate to seek additional help. Speaking to friends, family, or professionals isn't a sign of weakness; it's an extension of your self-care, reinforcing your resilience and well-being.

## APPLYING THE LEARNING

Based on what you've read in this chapter, ask yourself the following questions:

- What have you learned?
- What are your areas of growth?
- How will you apply your learnings from this chapter?

And then go a little deeper. Please be very specific.

- What two or three things are you going to start doing? _____
- What two or three things are you going to stop doing? _____
- What two or three things do you already do that you can build on? _____

## Self-Reflection Questions

1. What does self-care currently look like in my life? How am I prioritizing my well-being?
2. How regularly do I engage in activities that rejuvenate and refresh me, mentally physically and spiritually, and what are these activities?
3. How do I balance my commitment to my professional responsibilities with my personal life and well-being? Are there areas where I am overextending myself? Where might I need to adjust to maintain a healthier balance?
4. What are my early warning signs that I am experiencing stress or burnout? How do I typically respond to these signs, and what proactive steps can I take to address them before they escalate?
5. How am I modeling for my team that I take self-care seriously?

# 8
# Your Support System: Finding Strength in Community

*Life is not a solo act. It's a huge collaboration, and we all need to assemble around us the people who care about us and support us in times of strife.*

TIM GUNN

Being a leader can often feel like a lonely endeavor. You are in a position of significant influence and responsibility and are likely hesitant to show uncertainty or indecision, fearing it could undermine your authority or change perceptions of your competence. Your reluctance likely stems from organizational notions that equate leadership with infallible knowledge and unwavering strength, perpetuating the misconception that asking for help is a sign of weakness. I have also often heard from women leaders that the higher they climb the corporate ladder, the fewer peers they tend to have, which makes it even more challenging to identify individuals who can relate to your specific leadership challenges.

This sense of isolation can make it difficult to know whom to trust and confide in, leading to further emotional isolation. But the truth is that no leader can successfully operate in a vacuum. Support is imperative because it provides a confidential space for open dialogue, allowing leaders to explore challenges, brainstorm solutions, and gain perspective without the risk of judgment or exposure. Whether it's the sage advice from a mentor, the psychological insights from a therapist, or the practical strategies from a coach, each pillar of your support system plays a crucial role in your development and well-being.

Support enables you to navigate challenges, optimize your skills and abilities, establish a system of accountability, and creates a foundation for your resilience and emotional well-being. It multiplies your leadership capacity and opens your eyes to fresh, diverse viewpoints, leading to transformative solutions and averted missteps. Such support is a fundamental element for growth and sustainable leadership.

Leadership entails complexities and choices that often overwhelm even the most seasoned among us. The collective wisdom of your support system provides not just solutions but also serves as a reality check. After all, none of us have all the answers, and sometimes the most strategic move is simply asking for support. It brings an amalgam of perspectives into your orbit, thereby enriching your decision-making process, and it creates a culture where the contributions of others are not just recognized but actively sought.

As I have mentioned throughout this book, we all have unconscious biases and conditioned stereotypes and assumptions floating around in our minds, even if we aren't aware of them. Because we may not be aware, we need others in our support network to help us take notice.

Let me tell you a quick story to illustrate why this is so important.

A few years ago, I co-facilitated a workshop for young leaders at a very large company. After the workshop, several people stayed behind, many discussing the biases they have encountered in their interactions with other people at the company. Then, one young woman told us that she was in an interview process for a promotion and had been waiting to hear whether or not she had gotten the job. The day before our workshop, she had stopped by the office of the male senior manager who was hiring for the position and asked if he had made his decision yet. He told her that she had made it to the final group, and she was one of two people he was choosing from. He added, "It's so difficult! You're both so beautiful, I don't know how I am going to choose." She said she felt gutted and sick to her stomach and wasn't sure she wanted the promotion anymore if it meant working for this person.

Now, if I asked this man if he thought he did anything inappropriate, he'd likely say, no. He probably thought he was being charming and funny. He seemingly had no idea his comment was wildly inappropriate and a transparent reflection of his biases. He also had no idea the *impact* his statement had on this woman.

The point is, you may not be aware of your biases; and I am quite certain you are unaware of how much your biases impact your interactions with others, including how you treat your colleagues and team members. And, while it's essential to put in the work ourselves to identify and undo these thought patterns, most people need an objective support person to help them make real progress because the blind spots are a challenge to see by yourself.

Doing this work usually takes time and trust and requires assistance from professionals like coaches (and therapists). These experts can help illuminate what you don't see and give you the tools to dismantle these beliefs and biases. Furthermore, their input can stimulate lasting change, offering clarity on issues you might not have been able to discern on your own.

# UNDERSTANDING THE BENEFITS OF A SUPPORT SYSTEM

In addition to helping you steer through the myriad of challenges that leadership presents, your support network serves another crucial function: it opens the door to new possibilities and perspectives you might not have considered otherwise. The people in your support community circle can act as mirrors, reflecting not just who you are right now, but also who you could someday become. They elevate your thinking, offer constructive criticism, and even inspire creative approaches to long-standing problems.

They could also help you...

## Seek an outside perspective

In the fast-paced world of business, it's extremely easy to find ourselves enveloped in our own cognitive bubble. The constant pressures and decisions of the role can lead to a type of mental automation—patterns of thinking that grow rigid over time, like well-worn paths in our minds. We begin to see our challenges, relationships, and even our self-worth through a fixed lens. It's almost like being blinkered and only able to see a single option with no ability to see the periphery. This mental inflexibility can cloud judgment, inhibit creativity, and ultimately impact our performance and well-being.

The remedy? Inviting an outside perspective into our world. Engaging in open dialogues with trusted advisors can provide invaluable insights that disrupt our mental blinkeredness. An external viewpoint can highlight overlooked opportunities, present alternative solutions, and even reshape the way we perceive our own worth and abilities. It's the equivalent of opening a window in a stuffy room—it allows fresh air to circulate, rejuvenating our mental environment and offering clarity, especially on those days when the challenges seem insurmountable.

## Tackle difficult situations

Having a reliable support system is invaluable when confronting unfamiliar challenges or uncertainties in your professional or personal life. While obstacles are integral to our growth and learning, they often require effort and strategy to navigate effectively. The people in your support network serve different but equally important roles. Some may be great listeners, offering you a safe and confidential space to vocalize your concerns or frustrations, which is often the first step in problem-solving. Others may serve as drivers of positive change, providing you with the self-assurance and optimistic outlook essential for confronting challenges directly.

Besides, members of your professional support system— like mentors, coaches, or even sponsors—can provide actionable advice rooted in experience. They've likely navigated similar hurdles before and can offer a roadmap for overcoming them. This emotional and practical support combination equips you with a comprehensive toolkit for facing any challenge. Far from being a sign of weakness, leaning on your support system is a strategic move that can provide you with an edge, making the path through obstacles more maneuverable and the lessons learned more impactful.

## Be accountable

Embarking on a journey of self-discovery often requires more than individual effort—it benefits greatly from a robust support system. Developing and nurturing relationships with those who can hold you accountable can be invaluable. Accountability is a powerful motivator, transforming abstract goals into concrete actions. When you have someone to answer to, be it a coach, colleague, or friend, you're more likely to stay committed to your objectives. It provides an extra layer of responsibility that can be the difference between aspiration and actualization.

## OVERCOMING STIGMA

Navigating the complexities of personal and professional life can often make us feel like we're walking a tightrope. When we're grappling with these challenges, there's an unfortunate but pervasive stigma associated with asking for support. It's time to set the record straight: seeking assistance is not an admission of weakness; rather, it demonstrates self-awareness and the wisdom to seek improvement.

When clients come to me on the brink of burnout, wrestling with the elusive balance between work and personal well-being, I assure them they've already taken the first and most crucial step towards reaching that goal. By acknowledging the need for help, they've essentially already invested in their future. Being willing to learn from the expertise of others provides more than immediate relief—it also equips you with the skills and perspectives that serve you long-term. This kind of engagement is more than just problem-solving; it's an investment in your own growth and development.

Besides personal growth and development, effective leadership demands addressing immediate challenges that can affect team dynamics and productivity. This is when having a network of trusted peers and mentors becomes invaluable, offering both a confidential space for self-reflection and practical insights for the issues you face in real-time. In essence, two heads are often better than one, especially when confronting significant challenges.

Suppose you find yourself in a newly appointed leadership role but are struggling with team engagement or rallying colleagues behind your vision. This can quickly erode your motivation and enthusiasm, impacting not just you but your entire team. You may feel embarrassed about asking for help, not wanting anyone to see your challenges. But in reality, turning to a friend in a similar role can provide practical insights and alternative viewpoints and challenge your assumptions. Their lived experience can provide not just empathy but actionable advice.

Alternatively, consulting professionals like leadership consultants or executive coaches offers another layer of expertise. They bring to the table a wealth of experience, tailored strategies, and proven solutions that can address your specific challenges. These experts have encountered similar issues numerous times, equipping them with a toolkit of strategies to help you successfully navigate your situation.

# BUILDING UP A SUPPORT BASE

When we talk about "support," the term is intentionally broad because the world of individuals who can offer guidance, insight, or a listening ear is diverse. For some, your circle of support might readily come to mind, filled with people who have your back in times of professional or personal difficulty. Others may find that identifying those key individuals requires a bit more reflection.

Start by asking yourself who currently comprises your support base?

On a personal level, your inner circle may include family, close friends, or significant others who have been long-term constants in your life. These individuals often offer a stable foundation, providing comfort, encouragement, and emotional sustenance that bolsters your confidence and self-belief.

Professionally, you have an array of options: mentors who guide you, sponsors who advocate for you at work, coaches who sharpen your skills, therapists who offer psychological insights, and colleagues and managers who work with you day in and day out, offering their perspectives. Each plays a unique role, serving different facets of your professional growth and well-being.

And don't overlook the potential support that can come from more peripheral networks. Acquaintances, or friends of friends, people you frequently encounter in social settings like the gym, or mentors from your past, such as teachers who left an impression—these individuals can sometimes offer surprisingly valuable perspectives or opportunities. Being open and communicative in your social interactions can turn casual encounters into meaningful relationships.

The key is to actively cultivate this network of support. A robust support base isn't just a fallback for challenging times; it's a dynamic community of people who provide various forms of guidance, validation, and encouragement. While you may already have a reliable set of individuals in your corner, remember that networks are not static. There's always room for enrichment and expansion. Taking deliberate steps to deepen existing relationships and forge new connections can make your support base even more resilient and multidimensional. It is also crucial that your support is well-rounded and includes people who feel comfortable enough to tell you the hard truths you may not want to hear, and not simply agree with everything you say. You cannot grow as a leader surrounded by an echo chamber.

## Join a relevant club or community group

Being around like-minded people in your field can help you form bonds with people who have similar interests and may be more likely to understand when and how you need support in the future. Finding a community where you feel like you belong can provide you with peers that you feel really connected to and make you feel a genuine sense of shared purpose and mutual support.

## Network with people at work

We all fall into the trap of only speaking to the same people at work—our inner circle—the people we work with every day and no one else. But what about those within the business who you don't speak to often, or know that well, but could support you as you progress through the different levels in your career? Seek them out and ask them to meet for coffee or lunch for a chat. Even if you are a remote or hybrid worker you can still do this. You can either meet up on the day(s) you are in the office or decide to meet over video conferencing for a coffee, lunch, or just for a chat. Using instant messaging services isn't a good conduit for building relationships.

## Introduce yourself to others

This can be while you're socializing, having a coffee in a cafe, walking the dog, or exercising at the gym—try to be open to meeting new people and learning more about them. We introverts may cringe at the thought of this, but taking the risk and making yourself feel a little "uncomfortable" sometimes can pay off. Listen, I get it, I am introvert as well. But as much as I enjoy my quiet, alone time, I am fully aware how important it is to socialize with others and connect, so I have been practicing this myself. For me, I intentionally had to begin meeting and socializing with people who live in the same apartment building, and while I am out walking my dog. And, it has been great fun to hear about the life and career backgrounds of a very diverse group of people. Some are entrepreneurs and business owners, others are senior leaders in large corporate organizations, still others work for non-profit organizations, and others are retired. But they all bring such a wealth of knowledge and inspiration that enrich my life and my work.

So, build up your support base; it will be there for you through the different challenges life and work may throw at you.

# MENTORING, COACHING, AND SPONSORING

Mentors, coaches, and sponsors all act with the goal of helping people progress in their career. Each serves a unique function that can propel you from competency to mastery in your field.

However, each does it in a slightly different way.

## Mentoring

Mentors serve as seasoned guides, offering more than just technical know-how. Drawing from their experience, they provide real-world guidance, stories, and advice and even reveal valuable shortcuts, usually because they are in the same field as their mentees. Mentors can address multiple aspects of the mentee's life, including career, personal growth, and work-life balance. The relationship and schedule are typically less structured than coaching, with meetings arranged as needed and conversations covering a wide range of topics.

## Coaching

With coaching, the approach is less about the coach imparting wisdom and more about facilitating self-discovery. Unlike mentors, who draw on their own experience to guide you, coaches generally engage you with open-ended questions designed to help you find your own path forward. They challenge your thought patterns and provide the support needed to confront any limiting beliefs you may have. Now, this doesn't mean they don't offer suggestions or help you strategize or brainstorm ideas. But they should not be spending session after session telling you what to do or talking about themselves.

While coaching arrangements can be either short-term or long-term, they are often tightly focused on specific goals or developmental areas. A skilled coach offers specific feedback that shines a light on your blind spots, allowing you to refine your approach and improve performance. Operating under the conviction that you already possess the answers you seek, a coach's primary role is to guide you in unearthing those insights. This process doesn't just help with immediate issues; it also provides you with the tools to navigate future challenges more effectively.

## Sponsoring

Sponsors go beyond the roles of mentors and coaches by being your advocate in spaces where decisions about your career are made. They have both the influence and willingness to endorse you for opportunities. Unlike mentors, who act as guides, or coaches, who act as facilitators, sponsors are more like agents in the business world. They put their own reputation on the line for you and are highly invested in your success. Because of their high level of involvement, a sponsor's support can significantly accelerate your career trajectory. This is not a casual commitment; it's a deep, strategic partnership that can change the course of your professional life.

## Which one to choose?

In determining whether a mentor, coach, or sponsor is the right fit, you must first clarify your own specific needs and objectives. Are you looking for someone who can guide you based on their own professional journey, providing real-world advice and insights? A mentor would be ideal in this situation. However, if your aim is more about self-discovery, questioning your own limiting beliefs, and stretching your capabilities, then a coach would be more appropriate. Coaches facilitate your growth by letting you find your own solutions, rather than offering prescriptive advice. If you're at a point in your career where you have the skills and experience but lack the necessary visibility or connections to move up, a sponsor could be your best bet. They can open doors, make introductions, and advocate for you in rooms where decisions are made.

Each type of support comes with its own dynamics and expectations. A mentor is often someone from your field whose style or career path you admire; coaching is generally a more formal, often paid relationship with goals and, sometimes, a set timeline; a sponsor is someone who's willing to invest their reputation to help advance your career. Evaluate where you are in your career, where you want to go, and what gaps you need to fill to get there. This will help you determine which type of support is best suited to your current challenges and future aspirations.

## How coaches help you become a better leader

As you climb the ranks in your career, the demands and responsibilities can grow exponentially. The skills and traits that helped you excel in your previous roles may not be sufficient to navigate the complexities and challenges of leadership. In these times, hiring a coach can be a transformative decision. Leadership coaching is tailored to help senior professionals fine-tune their capabilities, both for themselves and their teams. It's an investment in sharpening crucial competencies like effective communication, decision-making, and strategic planning.

Leadership coaching doesn't just stop at individual development; it also extends to improving your interactions with your team. The focus often includes strengthening communication skills, building cohesive teams, and enhancing overall business performance. It serves as a tool to draw out your potential, helping you lead with more insight, influence, and effectiveness. The coach acts as a sounding board and a strategic partner, someone who challenges your thinking, raises your awareness, and helps you achieve your professional best.

The return on investment can be staggering. For example, a Fortune 500 company reported a 788% return on investment from their executive coaching program, which included a significant reduction in employee turnover.[36] This is a testament to the transformative power of coaching at the highest levels of an organization when there is a solid organizational commitment to the process.

For more than a decade, as a leadership and executive coach, I have had the opportunity to support my clients through key moments in their professional journeys. This role holds significant importance for me because the growth and decisions they make during these key moments has a meaningful impact on them as an individual, and ripple effects on their families, their teams, and their organization.

One major aspect of my work centers on supporting leaders with refining team dynamics because talent alone doesn't equate to team success. This involves exploring with leaders why their teams, despite high individual competencies, fail to deliver collectively. By identifying factors such as trust (with all its underlying elements), psychological safety, and inclusivity as central issues they can then begin taking action to address these core areas. Once leaders commit to their personal growth and improve their self-awareness, self-management, and communication skills, they are better positioned to execute targeted team-building exercises and facilitate open dialogue. They are able to work together better with their teams.

Leaders at all levels can struggle. Burnout is a harsh reality in today's workforce, particularly for high performers. Take the case of Melissa, a senior executive I coached. She came to me exhausted, fed up, and disengaged. She was putting in long hours, caught in a perpetual cycle of "just one more task," and it was taking a toll on both her performance and well-being. We worked on her self-awareness and self-management skills to better manage her stress responses and her relationship management and active listening skills to facilitate better interactions with her team members. We also implemented practical self-care strategies focused on improving her physical and mental well-being. This included boundary-setting exercises that empowered her to say "no" when necessary and take control of her time. We also took a deep dive into communication because Melissa was a brilliant strategist but found it challenging to articulate her vision in an easily digestible way for her team. She practiced listening to understand, being very specific when giving instructions, and having transparent conversations, especially in times of conflict. This work helped Melissa regain her drive and energy and gave her the tools to maintain a healthier work-life balance.

So, here's more of how coaches can support you:

## They show you how to reflect with more curiosity

Coaching is a great way for leaders to learn more about self-awareness—it's one of the biggest benefits a leadership coach can offer. It's no secret that leaders can experience issues in the workplace due to the inaccurate assumptions they make about those around them. This may even cause them to lose employees or create tension among them. A coach can provide a confidential safe space for a leader to work on eliminating the assumptions or biases they may have.

Throughout the coaching process, leaders are encouraged to observe how they lead themselves—including looking at how they think, what they believe, and the goals they set for themselves. Often this deeply curious reflection uncovers truths that they hadn't even considered.

## They empower you to take risks and build your confidence

A coach cannot "give" you confidence. But they are an instrumental resource to support you with fully comprehending and leveraging your unique abilities, which in turn, helps you develop more confidence. Confidence comes from doing the things you aren't sure you can do and either learning and growing from the experience or succeeding. Many leaders might not be fully aware of their distinct strengths or how best to utilize them. Through targeted coaching, leaders can gain keen insights into their skill sets and learn how to capitalize on them effectively. This self-empowerment is far-reaching; it boosts not only the leader's self-confidence—which research from Tallinn University associates with the attainment of high-level goals—but it also enriches the entire team by enhancing engagement and elevating productivity.[37]

## They encourage you to cultivate work-life balance for greater satisfaction

The relentless grind of working 12-hour days, skipping breaks and meals, and staying tethered to email long after office hours is a disturbingly common scenario for many leaders. In fact, the International Global Leadership Forecast 2021 revealed that, out of 15,000 surveyed leaders, nearly 60% reported feeling "used up" at the end of their work day, a clear indication of looming burnout.[38]

Coaches provide a vital perspective that allows leaders to reassess both their professional and personal lives. By taking a step back to evaluate their work habits, leadership styles, and overall well-being, leaders often find that they can improve not only their own performance but also that of their team. This holistic approach invariably leads to increased job satisfaction and a healthier work environment for all. Most importantly, this reflective pause allows leaders to make necessary adjustments, reducing the risk of burnout and fostering a more sustainable leadership model.

## They help you refine your communication skills

Leaders are often grappling with the complex art of communication. They may find themselves habitually resorting to knee-jerk reactions—expressing irritation when faced with a delayed project or frustration over a poorly structured presentation. These habitual reactions can stifle team engagement and even build barriers to open dialogue.

Through coaching, leaders can learn and practice new skills to move beyond their entrenched communication patterns that have formed over many years. This shift enhances not only individual leadership but also the broader team dynamics.

I want you to think about your community. How big is it? How helpful is it? And, how big of a role can it play in your career? Who is in your inner circle? Who can support you right now, in this moment?

## APPLYING THE LEARNING

Based on what you've read in this chapter, ask yourself the following questions:

- What have you learned?
- What are your areas of growth?
- How will you apply your learnings from this chapter?

And then go a little deeper. Please be very specific.

- What two or three things are you going to start doing? _____
- What two or three things are you going to stop doing? _____
- What two or three things do you already do that you can build on? _____

## Self-Reflection Questions

1. What are the signs that indicate I need assistance or guidance at work, and how comfortable am I in seeking help?
2. What is my long-term vision for my career, and how do my current commitments and consistent efforts align with achieving this vision? What additional supports might I need to add to my circle to help me reach my goals?
3. Who currently comprises my support system or network at work, and how do these individuals contribute to my professional growth and well-being? How often do I seek out their opinions, and how do I respond and act upon the feedback they provide?
4. Are there gaps in my network that I need to fill, particularly with people who can offer me honest, constructive feedback?

# 9

# Standing Strong: Harnessing Resilience in Leadership's Toughest Moments

*Your life is not determined by how you start the race but by the roadmap you use to get to the finish line, your willingness and ability to get back up when you fall, and your determination to get back on track when you lose your way.*

Resilience equips you to recover effectively from life's challenges, setbacks, and outright adversities. It's a dynamic set of skills developed over time as we navigate difficulties, adapt to changing circumstances, and demonstrate flexibility in the face of stress or uncertainty. I visualize it as "bouncing back," almost like an elastic band does when it's stretched to its limit and is then released.

Being resilient doesn't mean you don't have any emotional response to the event or circumstance. What it does mean is that you have a set of tools and skills that assist you with coping with the emotional distress caused by whatever is happening. The key is to utilize these skills to cope effectively and to not be mired in the emotion for so long as to feel helpless or hopeless about getting back on track.

You see, often resilience is confused with being "strong." But being resilient and being strong are not the same thing. When people say, "be strong," it's often the case that they're uncomfortable with your emotions—they don't want to see you be sad or express how you feel. Most often I have heard those words said when someone is very sad, and crying would be the normal emotion to express. So "be strong" has become synonymous with "don't cry" and perpetuates the myth that showing emotion is a sign of weakness. It isn't.

Expressing your emotions authentically and appropriately requires courage and self-awareness. Resilience emphasizes your ability to recover, without dismissing your emotional experiences. The time required for this recovery varies, influenced by the severity of the adversity faced. It's perfectly acceptable if it takes you longer to regain your footing, particularly if the experience was traumatic. Seeking external support is not a failure; it's an acknowledgment that we are human and sometimes need help to move forward.

Something worth addressing here is the discourse around whether encouraging resilience is encouraging toxic positivity—the idea that you keep pushing relentlessly through challenges while maintaining a positive mindset, without acknowledging how you are really feeling. Toxic positivity rejects all difficult emotions in favor of a cheerful and often falsely positive mask. But I don't agree that encouraging resilience is encouraging a denial of the full range of your emotions. I'm not talking about resilience in the same vein as, "Suck it up and just keep going no matter how you feel." That's not this. Acknowledging your feelings must always happen. You can be strong, and be resilient, and appropriately express your emotions.

In today's fast-paced world, leaders will face no shortage of challenges. From tight budgets and internal organizational conflicts to rapid market changes, the obstacles can feel relentless. What sets exceptional leaders apart isn't just intelligence or skill—it's resilience. This is the ability to adapt, recover, and grow stronger from difficulties. Resilience isn't an inherent trait that you are simply born with, but it is influenced by genetic factors.[39] It's a set of cultivated skills that are refined over time through experiences, across the continuum of positive experiences and tough challenges. As leaders, understanding the foundation of resilience can greatly assist in nurturing it within yourself and your team.

Its framework is deeply rooted in a blend of adaptability, self-awareness, and growth mindset.

Resilience can also equip you to successfully navigate challenging work environments effectively. A US study underscores this point by revealing that individuals with high levels of resilience perform better under stress, thereby not only enhancing their own well-being but also contributing to a healthier work culture.[40] This makes sense, as resilience isn't a temporary measure you employ when faced with adversity; it's a sustained mindset that informs your entire approach to work. While resilience enables you to operate effectively in high-stress scenarios, it's crucial to recognize that consistently working in such an environment isn't advisable or sustainable (without a lot of strategies for support in place).

# WHAT DO YOU DO WHEN LIFE THROWS YOU A CURVEBALL?

Picture this: you're hiking up an unfamiliar mountain. Despite your best intentions and the map in your hand, you lose your way and suffer a minor injury. At this moment, you're faced with a decision that can serve as a metaphor for your leadership journey. Do you abandon the climb, or recalibrate and continue upward? At various altitudes of this imaginary mountain, you would face different challenges—from unpredictable weather conditions to your own physical limitations. This mirrors the leadership landscape, replete with its own set of diverse challenges. And it's not just you—your team relies on your resilience skills and decision-making ability at each twist and turn.

Choices like these echo the kinds of decisions leaders have to make regularly. Whether it's confronting project setbacks, navigating team conflicts, or even laying off staff, you're faced with moments that test your resilience. When things don't go as planned—which they often don't—it's easy to question your next steps. This cycle of action, disappointment, reflection, and renewed action is constant.

The theme of bouncing back has been a long thread throughout my life. Take my academic career as an example. As I have mentioned before, I was faced with a series of challenging setbacks, almost resulting in my expulsion from my doctoral psychology program. This was a very steep, almost insurmountable cliff. My resilience toolkit in this instance consisted of support from mentors, family members, close friends, and my therapist, along with lots of extra study and clinical hours, and many moments of reflection. Transcending this set of obstacles and coming through on the other side didn't just solidify my academic standing but also enriched my holistic understanding of resilience. I made it through. You can probably imagine the intense emotions I felt being in the auditorium, when I walked across the stage, was "hooded," and got my diploma. I did it!

I'm not saying that setbacks don't affect me anymore. But I have developed a versatile set of tools for dealing with challenges. And this toolkit is ever-evolving because, in reality, you may need different tools for different circumstances. It's filled with stress management techniques, emotional regulation skills, and the ability to communicate clearly, especially under pressure. Resilience isn't about immediate recovery, but it is about not losing sight of your long-term goals and having the perseverance to move towards them, regardless of the speed.

Sometimes, when you work for yourself, as I do, the challenges are seemingly endless. Projects don't always go as planned, you may have challenging clients (but my clients aren't), things take much longer than expected, and market conditions can change without notice. Each obstacle demanding almost instantaneous decisions. Through all of these challenges, you may find yourself wondering as I have, "Now what?" For me, though, the answer has always been rooted in resilience: adapt, persist, and maintain the conviction that I'll always find my way.

Your ability to bounce back is a skill set you cultivate over time, one that evolves as you do. Whenever I find myself doubting my ability to handle a situation, I remind myself that resilience is not innate but learned. I've worked hard to cultivate this trait, and you can too.

As a leader, you will be faced with a wide range of challenges that can derail even the most well-laid plans. Your innovative ideas might not gain traction, leaving you back at square one. Mistakes—whether they're yours or your team's—can create significant roadblocks. Then there are external factors like budget cuts or a high-performing employee's sudden exit that add another layer of complexity. Market shifts or new regulations can demand rapid changes, forcing you into reactive mode. Operational glitches, from technology meltdowns to failed project launches, can consume your focus and resources. Interpersonal conflicts or breakdowns in communication can escalate quickly, demanding sensitive and immediate intervention. Layoffs present a particularly agonizing challenge, filled with emotional and practical ramifications for both the departing employees and the remaining team. Customer complaints or issues can also surface at any time, requiring prompt and thoughtful solutions to safeguard your company's reputation. Each of these challenges can ripple through your team and organization, impacting morale, productivity, and your bottom line.

Resilience becomes your guiding compass through this array of leadership challenges. When an idea doesn't gain traction, resilience allows you to reevaluate and pivot without succumbing to discouragement. Mistakes become opportunities for growth, not just for you but also for your team. When external pressures like budget cuts or market shifts arise, a resilient mindset focuses on adaptability and efficient resource allocation. During operationally challenging times, such as technology failures or project setbacks, resilience helps you keep a level head, emphasizing problem-solving and immediate course correction. And, should you face the painful task of laying off staff, resilience supports you in making those difficult decisions with both compassion and pragmatism, while using kindness and empathy to have those conversations with the team members directly impacted. It also prepares you for the emotional toll of the changes and equips you to bolster the morale of the remaining team members. In the face of customer complaints or issues, resilience encourages a proactive approach to conflict resolution, preserving both the relationship and your company's reputation.

Ultimately, resilience helps you proactively build a workplace culture that is robust, adaptable, and psychologically safe, thereby minimizing the negative impact of these challenges on team morale and performance.

## WHAT DOES HIGH OR LOW RESILIENCE LOOK LIKE?

Resilience isn't a static quality; it's more like a muscle that needs consistent exercise to maintain its strength. You may have phases in your life where you feel particularly resilient and able to handle whatever challenges come your way with grace and agility. However, this can change due to a variety of factors. For instance, enduring high levels of stress over an extended period of time can deplete your coping capacity, making it harder to bounce back. Similarly, personal life events—such as the loss of a loved one, a breakup, or other significant traumas—can overwhelm your emotional reserves, leading to periods of lower resilience.

Recognizing when you're in a phase of diminished resilience is crucial. Without a strong set of coping skills, it's easy to fall into patterns that exacerbate the issue. This doesn't mean you've failed; it simply means you're human. But ignoring these signs can lead you down a risky path, potentially causing you to engage in maladaptive coping strategies like substance abuse or other unhealthy behaviors as a way to manage your emotions. It's important to remember that these are temporary solutions to a deeper issue and will likely create more problems in the long run. The aim is to identify these low-resilience periods and take proactive steps to rebuild your emotional toolkit, whether that means seeking professional help, leaning on your support network, or adopting new coping techniques.

\* If your low resilience period feels like it is lasting beyond a couple of weeks and you feel like your coping skills and normal self-care is not enough, please seek professional help.

How can you identify whether you are in a low or high resilience period?

Ask yourself: what comes to mind when something goes wrong?

If you are having a low resilience day, you may…

- Have the feeling that it's the end of the world.
- Have panic set in.
- Start placing blame on other people or feel like a victim.
- Avoid looking for opportunities for growth.
- Feel down and disappointed.
- React irritably or impulsively to situations.

If you are having a high resilience day, you may…

- Respond to the situation with curiosity and calmness, rather than reacting impulsively.
- Have a sense of control over the situation or release control if warranted.
- Use your self-care strategies to deal positively with stressful situations.
- Know that this isn't the end of the world.
- Be willing to work on what you can do to get back on track again.

# DEVELOPING YOUR COMMITMENT TO GROWTH

To truly stand strong and harness resilience during some of your more challenging moments as a leader, it will do wonders for you to develop a true commitment to growth. Having that capacity to embrace challenges rather than fear them will set you apart—and give you the momentum to persist even when you face setbacks.

An integral aspect of your journey is the mindset with which you approach these challenges and opportunities. Introduced in 2006 in a book called *Mindset* by psychologist Dr. Carol Dweck, the concept of a growth mindset revolves around the idea that abilities and intelligence are attributes that can be honed and developed over time.[41] This contrasts sharply with a fixed mindset, where individuals believe that their capabilities are predetermined and unalterable.

In the realm of leadership, adopting a growth mindset becomes an invaluable asset. It's not merely about showcasing your intelligence or talent; rather, it thrives on the pillars of continuous learning, adaptation, and the relentless pursuit of improvement through effort. Through this lens, leaders start to see challenges not as insurmountable obstacles, but as opportunities for growth and development.

This shift in perspective is vital when cultivating resilience. Resilience, after all, is the ability to navigate setbacks, adapt to unforeseen changes, and maintain steadfastness in the face of adversity. If you are grounded in a growth mindset you will view failures and setbacks as lessons, rather than definitive judgments of your capabilities. You will have a better understanding that encountering and overcoming obstacles are pivotal moments on your trajectory towards success.

However, the alternative, a fixed mindset, can pose significant hurdles. When faced with challenges, if you are anchored in this mindset, you may interpret these challenges as a direct critique of your inherent abilities. Instead of seeking lessons from setbacks, you risk becoming disheartened or may even choose to avoid difficult tasks, fearing the sting of potential failure. This mindset not only stalls your personal and professional growth but also weakens your resilience, making it challenging to steer through the inevitable storms.

In the demanding world of business, where challenges are abundant and stakes are high, resilience is invaluable. Fostering a growth mindset is not merely a personal development strategy; it's essential for empowering leaders to navigate complex roles and emerge stronger from their experiences.

This is a snapshot of what to look out for:

- FIXED:
    - A "fixed mindset" assumes that our character, intelligence, and creative ability are given at birth and governed by genetics.
    - Sees abilities as static, which can't change in any meaningful way.
    - Views success as the affirmation of that inherent intelligence.
    - Thinks challenges are frustrating and to be avoided.
    - Striving for success and avoiding failure at all costs becomes a way of maintaining the sense of being smart or skilled.
    - Thinks "I'm so stupid because I don't know how to do that."
    - Will likely give up easily if it feels too hard and doesn't come effortlessly.
    - May feel threatened by the success of other people around them.

- GROWTH:
    - A "growth mindset" thrives on challenge.
    - Sees failure as a springboard for growth and for stretching our existing abilities.
    - Focuses on continuous improvement and self-awareness through ongoing feedback.
    - Believes our character, intelligence, and creative ability are things we can cultivate through our efforts/deliberate practice.
    - Change and growth come from application and experience.
    - Thinks, "This is cool. I am learning new ways of doing this."
    - Celebrates others' success.

As you can hopefully see, a growth mindset is essential for embracing challenges as opportunities and for navigating setbacks effectively. It's more than just putting in the effort; it's about intentional learning, self-awareness, and adaptability. To shift from a fixed to a growth mindset, engage in daily reflection. Make it an evening ritual—perhaps with a cup of tea in a calming environment—and consider the following questions:

- What did I learn today?
- What mistake taught me something valuable?
- Where did I invest significant effort?
- What habits should I cultivate to sustain my progress?
- What actionable steps can I take to succeed?
- Where can I find constructive feedback?
- Do I have clarity on my desired outcome?
- What additional information do I need, and where can I find it?

By asking yourself these questions, you move beyond the immediate challenges and focus on personal development and future opportunities. This reflective practice reinforces your resilience, helping you navigate difficult moments with greater ease.

## HOW ELSE CAN WE IMPROVE RESILIENCE?

Committing to a growth mindset is a pivotal first step in enhancing your resilience as a leader. However, it's important to recognize that resilience is multifaceted and can be further developed through various resources and skills that can be practiced and honed over time.

Here are some of those options:

### Feel what you feel

Being resilient means that when you experience a difficult situation, you experience the emotion (sadness or anger, perhaps) and are able to express it appropriately. You feel it, talk about it if you need to, and can move forward (which doesn't mean you won't have to revisit it in the future). We all experience challenging situations, so it's okay to admit that you feel disappointed with an outcome at work, or that something hasn't worked out as you expected. It's normal to feel like that, so it's important to acknowledge these feelings. Dismissing them won't do you any good. As you "bounce back," you continuously use your healthy coping skills to process and work through any roadblocks.

## Change your inner voice

Having positive self-talk is crucial in helping you build your resilience. Notice what you say to yourself in an unfamiliar or challenging situation—practice turning negatives into positives and being kind to yourself. Berating yourself with harsh words or telling yourself that you can't make that mistake again is not the recipe for a resilient character. We all make mistakes, and sometimes we make the same mistakes more than once. Each time explore what happened and what went wrong, give yourself some grace, and start to delve into what is a lesson learned from that situation, and what steps can be taken to move forward from there. You may even be able to identify how to avoid the misstep in the future.

For me, if a situation has an outcome that I am less than pleased with, after taking some time to process my thoughts and feelings, I look at myself in the mirror, take a very deep breath, and remind myself that I can make it through this successfully, like I always do, somehow. Each day, we get a new opportunity to demonstrate our resilience and resourcefulness.

## Maintain your focus on a long-term goal

Commitment to your long-term goals plays a vital role in developing resilience. This focused dedication provides you with a clear sense of direction, helping to guide your choices and actions. When you encounter disruptions or challenges, a strong sense of purpose enables you to adapt and realign your priorities, ensuring you stay on the path towards your objectives.

## Practice self-care

During exceptionally challenging times, self-care becomes even more critical, but also more basic. It might involve prioritizing sleep because a well-rested mind tackles challenges more effectively than a fatigued one. It could be setting aside just 10 minutes a day for a deep breathing or mindfulness exercise to help you have an emotion reset. Or maybe it's having a candid conversation with a trusted colleague or friend, not to seek solutions necessarily, but to simply be heard. It's not always about having an elaborate regimen but just making sure to take small but meaningful actions that preserve your well-being. When overwhelmed, even the act of writing down three things you're grateful for each day can shift your focus and lighten the emotional load.

In short, self-care during stressful times often boils down to the essentials: sleep, nourishment, emotional release, and a moment of mindfulness. These are the building blocks that help you stay resilient when facing challenges head-on.

The key message? Take time for yourself. And during this time, it's important to look after yourself. Don't beat yourself up about something—find your Zen, the thing that helps you feel calm, and embark on a journey of discovering more about yourself. This will also help you manage stress and anxiety levels.

## Learn to manage uncertainty

Learning to manage uncertainty is essential for effective leadership, especially when facing stressful circumstances. If you find yourself constantly catastrophizing or expecting the worst, take a step back. First, become aware of your thought patterns; recognize when you're drifting into pessimism. Ground yourself in facts rather than speculations of disaster and consider breaking complex challenges into smaller, manageable tasks. This approach not only focuses your energy on what's achievable but also builds your confidence, reducing the likelihood of catastrophic thinking.

Second, evaluate the actual likelihood of your worst-case scenarios, which often are far less probable than your mind might lead you to believe. Be honest. Lean into your network of trusted advisors for diverse perspectives, as they provide a more balanced understanding of the situation. Pair this with mindfulness practices to help you stay rooted in the present, and you'll find yourself better equipped to not jump to imagining disaster so quickly.

## Get comfortable asking for help

In Chapter 8, we discussed the importance of having a support system. To recap, being resilient doesn't mean you don't need help. It doesn't mean you don't need a therapist, family, or friends to be there for you. That's why maintaining healthy relationships with important people in your life is beneficial in building your resilience.

Getting support from a close friend, a family member, a coach, a therapist, or a counselor to assist you with coping with a challenging situation can be extremely useful in helping you build and maintain our resilience.

## Never, ever give up on yourself

Arguably the most important of them all. Always show up for yourself.

In this final chapter, we've explored the multifaceted domain of resilience, a muscle strengthened by mastering the skills discussed throughout this book. With these tools at your disposal, you're now well equipped to rebound from any adversity that comes your way. It's important to remember, though, that resilience isn't an innate trait but a skill set—one that you can, and indeed should, consistently nurture over time.

# APPLYING THE LEARNING

Based on what you've read in this chapter, ask yourself the following questions:

- What have you learned?
- What are your areas of growth?
- How will you apply your learnings from this chapter?

And then go a little deeper. Please be very specific.

- What two or three things are you going to start doing? _____
- What two or three things are you going to stop doing? _____
- What two or three things do you already do that you can build on? _____

## Self-Reflection Questions

1. How do I react to unexpected changes or disruptions in my work environment, and what strategies do I employ to adapt effectively?
2. How do I balance being consistent in my approach with the need to adapt and learn in a rapidly changing professional environment?
3. How do I foster resilience within my team? What practices do I implement to ensure my team feels supported and empowered to navigate and bounce back from workplace challenges?
4. How do I typically respond to setbacks or challenges in my leadership role? What strategies have I used to overcome these difficulties, and how can I further develop my resilience to better handle future challenges?

# Conclusion

*The enjoyment of life is all about the journey. If you stay focused on the end goal, you will miss out on all the fun!*

Being an exceptional leader is a journey of continual growth. In this book, I have mapped out the elements that I believe will contribute to your evolution as a leader—emotional intelligence, effective communication, unwavering commitment and consistency, diligent self-care, a supportive community, and the resilience to weather the storms. Each of these aspects feed into the core concept of resilience, which in turn strengthens your ability to lead. As you've hopefully seen, these aren't isolated skill sets but interlinked aspects that collectively enable you to navigate the complexities of leadership and a rapidly changing work environment.

Yet, evolution implies change, and change is constant. Just as you reach new heights, fresh challenges will emerge. That's where the real beauty of this book lies. As I said at the beginning of this book, it's not a one-time manual but an enduring guide. Every time you find yourself at a new crossroad, faced with novel issues or opportunities for growth, this book will offer you pertinent insights anew. Think of it as your go-to resource for every stage of your leadership journey.

The work of evolving, expanding, and elevating is never finished; it's an ongoing cycle of action, reflection, and growth. It's about not just solving today's problems but preparing yourself for future challenges that are, as of now, unknown. You build resilience not as an end in itself, but as a by-product of this relentless commitment to evolution.

In our unpredictable and uncertain world, where the only constant is change, your commitment to evolution isn't just a personal advantage—it's an organizational necessity. So, keep evolving, because every new version of you offers fresh perspectives, richer experiences, and greater resilience. And in that continual evolution, you'll find not just success but a deeper, more meaningful form of leadership.

So, as you close this book, keep it within arm's reach, because the tools, strategies, and mindsets encapsulated here will be just as relevant the next time you find yourself needing to adapt, change, or grow. The goal isn't just to survive the challenges that come your way but to thrive in the face of them, time and time again.

# Notes

[1] Daniel Goleman, *Emotional intelligence: Why it can matter more than IQ* (1995).

[2] N Dishon, "The effect of trait self-awareness, self-reflection, and perceptions of choice meaningfulness on indicators of social identity" (2017). Available from: www.frontiersin.org/articles/10.3389/fpsyg.2017.02034/full

[3] "What predicts executive success?" Cornell University's School of Industrial and Labor Relations (2019). Available from: www.amanet.org/articles/new-study-shows-nice-guys-finish-first/

[4] Donald Hebb, "The organization of behavior" (1949), via Hebbian Learning, The Decision Lab. Available from: https://thedecisionlab.com/thinkers/neuroscience/donald-hebb

[5] "New Year's goals," University of Scranton, via inc.com (2016). Available from: www.inc.com/marcel-schwantes/science-says-92-percent-of-people-dont-achieve-goals-heres-how-the-other-8-perce.html

[6] "American Trends Panel (ATP)," Pew Research Center (2020). Available from: www.pewresearch.org/our-methods/u-s-surveys/the-american-trends-panel/; "Managers account for 70% of variance in employee engagement," Gallup (2015). Available from: https://news.gallup.com/businessjournal/182792/managers-account-variance-employee-engagement.aspx

[7] "Earth is now our only shareholder," EU Patagonia (2022). Available from: www.patagonia.com/one-percent-for-the-planet.html

[8] Nora Gallagher and Lisa Myers, *Patagonia's tools for grassroots activists: Best practices for success in the environmental movement* (2016).

[9] George Doran, Arthur Miller, and James Cunningham, "There's a S.M.A.R.T. way to write management goals and objectives," *Management Review (1981).*

[10] "The world's workplace is broken—here's how to fix it," Gallup (2022). Available from: www.gallup.com/workplace/393395/world-workplace-broken-fix.aspx#:~:text=81%2C396%20hours.&text=The%20only%20thing%20we%20spend,work%20and%2019%25%20are%20miserable

[11] Stephen R. Covey, *The 7 habits of highly effective people* (revised edition 2020).

[12] "Humans are hardwired for connection? Neurobiology 101 for parents, educators, practitioners and the general public," Wellesley Centers for Women (2010). Available from: www.wcwonline.org/2010/humans-are-hardwired-for-connection-neurobiology-101-for-parents-educators-practitioners-and-the-general-public

[13] Daniel Goleman, *Emotional intelligence: Why it can matter more than IQ* (1995).

[14] "6 business icons who credit their success to neurodivergence," Uptimize. Available from: https://uptimize.com/neurodivergent-icons/

[15] Dr. Albert Mehrabian, 7-38-55 theory in *Silent Messages* (1971).

[16] Daniel Goleman and Richard E. Boyatzis, "Emotional intelligence has 12 elements. Which do you need to work on?" *Harvard Business Review* (2017). Available from: https://hbr.org/2017/02/emotional-intelligence-has-12-elements-which-do-you-need-to-work-on

[17] Dr. Albert Mehrabian, 7-38-55 theory in *Silent Messages* (1971).

[18] Interact/Harris Poll, *Harvard Business Review* (2015). Available from: https://hbr.org/2015/06/the-top-complaints-from-employees-about-their-leaders

[19] "Two thirds of managers are uncomfortable communicating with employees," *Harvard Business Review* (2016). Available from: https://hbr.org/2016/03/two-thirds-of-managers-are-uncomfortable-communicating-with-employees

[20] "Where Millennials end and Generation Z begins," Pew Research (2019). Available from: www.pewresearch.org/short-reads/2019/01/17/where-millennials-end-and-generation-z-begins/

[21] "Give performance reviews that actually inspire employees," Gallup (2017). Available from: https://news.gallup.com/opinion/gallup/219863/give-performance-reviews-actually-inspire-employees.aspx#:~:text=According%20to%20Gallup%2C%2026%25%20of,say%20they%20are%20reviewed%20annually

[22] "Why is recognition at work important?" PDF report, Gallup/Work Human (2022).

[23] Helen Riess, "The science of empathy," *Journal of Patient Experience* 4 (2), 74–77 (June 2017). Available from: www.ncbi.nlm.nih.gov/pmc/articles/PMC5513638/#:~:text=In%20the%20past%2C%20empathy%20was,taught%20to%20health%2Dcare%20providers

[24] Joseph Chancellor, Seth Margolis, Katherine Jacobs Bao, and Sonja Lyubomirsky, "Everyday prosociality in the workplace: The reinforcing benefits of giving, getting, and glimpsing," National Library of Medicine (2018). Available from: https://pubmed.ncbi.nlm.nih.gov/28581323/

25 "EY empathy in business survey," EY Consulting (2021). Available from: www.ey.com/en_us/news/2021/09/ey-empathy-in-business-survey
26 "Listening more difficult in today's digital workplace," Accenture (2016). Available from: https://newsroom.accenture.com/news/2015/accenture-research-finds-listening-more-difficult-in-todays-digital-workplace; "Effective listening by using awareness," *HR Magazine* (2018). Available from: www.hrmagazine.co.uk/content/features/effective-listening-by-using-awareness/#:~:text=You%20might%20be%20surprised%20to,problems%20and%20expand%20our%20understanding
27 Jaimar Tuarez, "How many words can the brain process per minute?" NeuroTray (2022). Available from: https://neurotray.com/how-many-words-can-the-brain-process-per-minute/
28 Simon Alexander Ong, *Energize: Make the most of every moment* (2022).
29 "Burn-out an 'occupational phenomenon': International classification of diseases," World Health Organization (2019). Available from: www.who.int/news/item/28-05-2019-burn-out-an-occupational-phenomenon-international-classification-of-diseases#:~:text=%E2%80%9CBurn%2Dout%20is%20a%20syndrome,related%20to%20one's%20job%3B%20and
30 "Workplace burnout survey," Deloitte (2015). Available from: www2.deloitte.com/us/en/pages/about-deloitte/articles/burnout-survey.html
31 "How self-care can help prevent burnout," Spring Health (2022). Available from: www.springhealth.com/blog/how-self-care-prevents-burnout#:~:text=That's%20a%20staggering%20statistic%2C%20and,%2C%20mental%2C%20and%20emotional%20wellbeing
32 "Survey shows 80% of US adults will be more mindful of practicing self-care post-pandemic," News, Medical Life Sciences (2020). Available from: www.news-medical.net/news/20200603/Survey-shows-8025-of-US-adults-will-be-more-mindful-of-practicing-self-care-post-pandemic.aspx
33 "Balancing act: Americans prioritize daily self-care, but struggle to keep up," Zenger (2023). Available from: www.zenger.news/2023/09/22/balancing-act-americans-prioritize-daily-self-care-but-struggle-to-keep-up/
34 "Benefits of Physical Activity," Center for Disease Control and Prevention (Last review 2023). Available from: www.cdc.gov/physicalactivity/basics/pa-health/index.htm#:~:text=Being%20physically%20active%20can%20improve,activity%20gain%20some%20health%20benefits
35 "Recommended amount of sleep for a healthy adult," American Academy of Sleep Medicine and Sleep Research Society (2015). Available from: www.ncbi.nlm.nih.gov/pmc/articles/PMC4434546/#:~:text=Current%20evidence%20supports%20the%20general,%2C%20medical%2C%20and%20environmental%20factors
36 Merrill C Anderson, "Case study on the return on investment of executive coaching." Available from: www.american.edu/provost/ogps/executive-education/executive-coaching/roi-of-executive-coaching.cfm

[37] "Leadership attributes: Trait approach," Tallin University (2009). Available from: www.tlu.ee/~sirvir/Leadership/Leadership%20 Attributes/selfconfidence.html#:~:text=Self%2Dconfidence%20is%20 necessary%20for,86

[38] "Global leadership forecast," DDI World (2021). Available from: www. ddiworld.com/global-leadership-forecast-2021

[39] Stephan Maul, Ina Giegling, Chiara Fabbri, Filippo Corponi, Alessandro Serretti, and Dan Rujescu. "Genetics of resilience: Implications from genome-wide association studies and candidate genes of the stress response system in posttraumatic stress disorder and depression," *American Journal of Medical Genetics. Part B Neuropsychiatric Genetics* 183 (2), 77–94 (March 2020). Available from: https:// pubmed.ncbi.nlm.nih.gov/31583809/#:~:text=Resilience%20 is%20undeniably%20influenced%20by,about%20the%20exact%20 underlying%20mechanisms

[40] Andrew Shatté, Adam Perlman, Brad Smith, and Wendy D. Lynch, "The positive effect of resilience on stress and business outcomes in difficult work environments," in *Journal of Occupational and Environmental Medicine*, 59 (2), 135–140 (February 2017). Available from: www.ncbi.nlm. nih.gov/pmc/articles/PMC5287440/

[41] Carol Dweck, *Mindset: How you can fulfil your potential* (updated version, 2012).

# Exercises

## EXERCISE 1

This exercise will help you identify your personal values. What do you value in your life and career? Your values are the beliefs you have that identify what is most important to you. They guide the choices you make. Knowing what your values are will help you recognize the parts of your life that might need some attention, and what you may want to prioritize for the future.

Circle the 10 most important items from the following list. Rank them from 1–10, with "1" being the most important item.

| | |
|---|---|
| ___ Love | ___ Time with Family |
| ___ Honesty | ___ Loyalty |
| ___ Wealth | ___ Morals |
| ___ Humor | ___ Knowledge |
| ___ Reason | ___ Spirituality |
| ___ Success | ___ Power |
| ___ Friendship | ___ Relaxation & Self-Care |
| ___ Fun Personal Time | ___ Freedom |
| ___ Adventure | ___ Independence |

| | |
|---|---|
| ___ Variety | ___ Nature |
| ___ Personal Achievement | ___ Respect |
| ___ Calmness | ___ Responsibility |
| ___ Recognition | ___ Wisdom |
| ___ Beauty | ___ Peace |
| ___ Popularity/Fame | ___ Stability |
| ___ Fairness/Justice | ___ Creativity |
| ___ Safety | ___ Health & Nutrition |
| ___ Philanthropy | ___ Financial Security |

---

My top five values I want to live by:

1. _____
2. _____
3. _____
4. _____
5. _____

The values my life currently reflects (the ones I actually live by):

1. _____
2. _____
3. _____
4. _____
5. _____

Now look at your top five again. If you could only choose three to live your life from for the next 12 months, what would they be?

1. _____
2. _____
3. _____

What is it about these three values that make them important choices for you right now?

_____

_____

_____

# EXERCISE 2

- What are the current everyday stressors (include work and personal life) that have you feeling overwhelmed, burned out, or frustrated? Make a list of them. Use the Thoughts/Feelings/Actions/Results process to identify what thoughts are triggering these feelings and what the ultimate results are. Then reverse engineer the process to see what you can change in order to adjust your inner experience.
- Take a moment to scan your body. Where in your body do you experience stress? Sadness? Anxiety? Anger/frustration? What does it feel like?
  o Examples: tightness in chest or throat; feeling hot; feeling short of breath; heart racing; fist and/or jaw clenching; headache/migraine
- Breathe. Take some slow, deep inhales and exhales to relax your body and mind. Do this for at least five minutes.
- Begin a gratitude journal. Each day, take some time to think about and write down the things you are grateful for.
  o Sample gratitude journal entry: I am grateful for... I appreciate that... I acknowledge... I am thankful that/for... _Words to avoid: can't, don't, won't, not, didn't._

# EXERCISE 3

Your answers to these questions will give you clues as to how you prepare for your day and whether or not your morning routine is working for you.

- How do you begin your day currently? What is your very first thought as you wake up in the morning? How do you feel? Tired? Sluggish? Energized? Excited? At what time of day do you feel fully awake and most alert?
- For the next week, have your first thought in the morning be, "Yes! I'm awake and alive and ready to have a wonderful day!" Then begin your day with a moment of gratitude (I am grateful/thankful for...). Then set your intention: Today is going to be _____ _____ ____. I will _____
- Each day write down in your daily journal what you notice about how you think, feel, and act after making these changes to your morning mental script. What *new* results are you seeing in your everyday life?

## EXERCISE 4

- Write down your top three or four "Negative Nelly" or "Critical Chris" statements and comments that you frequently make. Examples: I suck. This will never work. You always/never...

  1. _____
  2. _____
  3. _____
  4. _____

- Reframe your negative comments to something more positive and empowering. Examples: I can do this. I love myself. I am creative and innovative and can find solutions.
- For 24 hours consciously *stop* yourself from uttering the negative words to yourself and others. In 24 hours, how many times did you have to stop yourself from criticizing yourself and others? What did you notice? In your journal, reflect on how much you judge others and

yourself throughout the day. What would it be like to stop judging so much? Do you think this is possible for you?

## EXERCISE 5

- How does fear of rejection show up in your business/career/life? What does it stop you from doing?
- How does fear of humiliation show up in your business/career/life? What does it stop you from doing?
- How does fear of not being good enough show up in your business/career/life? What does it stop you from doing?
- How does fear of failure show up in your business/career/life? What does it stop you from doing?
- How does fear of success show up in your business/career/life? What does it stop you from doing?
- If you want to get unstuck, you *must* take action. What three steps can you start taking now to rewrite your inner scripts and show *fear* that you will not die as you grow outside your comfort zone.

1. _____
2. _____
3. _____

## EXERCISE 6

- What have you been avoiding? What behaviors do you practice so you avoid things? Procrastination? Distraction with social media, emails, phone calls?
- How are these behaviors holding you back?
- Write down two empowering mantras and look yourself in the eye in a mirror and say them... Then take deliberate action on something you have been avoiding.

1. _____
2. _____

# EXERCISE 7

Make your to-do and to-don't list

- For your to-do list, put a "1" next to things that you must do to reach a goal.
- For your to-don't list, put a "2" next to the items that are administrative/tech that would be better done by someone else.
- Put a "3" next to things that you hate doing and you take so long to do that it would be better if it were done by someone else.

| TASK LIST | 1, 2, or 3 |
|-----------|------------|
|           |            |
|           |            |
|           |            |

# EXERCISE 8

After four to six weeks of practicing your new habits, reflect on how things are going.

- In what ways are you still procrastinating and avoiding?
- Where did you get stuck? What stories are you *still* telling yourself that are not helpful?
- What new words are you using to replace negative ones?

# Emotion Vocabulary

**Sad:**
Melancholy
Downhearted
Despondent
Grief-stricken
Somber
Disheartened
Forlorn
Upset
Unhappy
Miserable
Gloomy
Despondent
Desolate

**Happy:**
Elated
Joyful
Jubilant
Ecstatic
Contented
Cheerful
Buoyant
Blissful

**Angry/Mad:**
Irate
Annoyed
Agitated
Incensed
Enraged
Fuming
Exasperated
Furious
Incensed

**Disappointed:**
Dismayed
Disenchanted
Disheartened
Crestfallen
Discouraged
Disillusioned
Downcast

**Frustrated:**
Aggravated
Irritated
Perturbed

Impatient
Annoyed
Vexed
Disgruntled

**Anxious/
Nervous:**
Apprehensive
Tense
Jittery
Uneasy
Edgy
Worried
Restless

**Excited:**
Thrilled
Exhilarated
Enthusiastic
Revved up
Charged
Pumped
Avid

**Confused:**
Perplexed
Baffled
Bewildered
Disoriented
Puzzled
Uncertain
Muddled

**Hopeful:**
Optimistic
Uplifted
Encouraged
Confident
Positive
Sanguine
Assured

**Overwhelmed:**
Swamped
Engulfed
Bombarded
Burdened
Besieged
Flooded
Snowed under

**Relieved:**
Alleviated
Comforted
Reassured
Soothed
Eased

Unburdened
Petrified
Scared
Timid

**Insecure:**
Uncertain
Self-Conscious
Doubtful
Timid
Hesitant
Anxious
Unsure

**Ashamed**
Embarrassed
Humiliated
Remorseful
Worthless
Unworthy
Guilty
Regretful
Mortified

**Afraid**
Terrified
Fearful
Anxious
Worried
Nervous
Panicky
Bitterness
Resentment

**Love**
Affection
Adore
Fancy
Appreciate
Fondness
Devotion
Passion

**Envy**
Jealousy
Greed
Spite
Lightened

**Surprise**
Astonishment
Amazement
Wonder
Disbelief
Shock
Flabbergasted
Stunned
Dumbfounded

**Energized**
Invigorated
Boosted
Motivated
Vibrant
Revitalized
Rejuvenated

# Acknowledgments

Embarking on the journey of writing this book has been a profound experience of personal growth and evolution for me. Each phase of this process has contributed significantly to my development as an author. I am deeply grateful for the myriad of people who have supported me, offering their insights and expertise to shape and refine the contents of this work.

First and foremost, I want to thank Amy Packham; without you, this book would still be waiting to be written. Thank you for the countless hours of collaborative brainstorming, revising, and editing the many words in this book! You really helped me determine what I wanted to say and get the structure right.

A special thank you to the early readers of this manuscript: Tracy Duhaney, Justin George, Amit Sirker, Julie Ennis, Sarah Pizzo, Kevin Cushnie, Cindy Rodriguez, Marcel Wright, and Andre Cromwell—your honest and insightful feedback was fundamental in shaping and refining the book's content. Your constructive critiques have been invaluable in improving the overall quality of this work. Thank you so very much.

To my family, thank you so much for your love and guidance. And, of course, a special shoutout to my wonderful daughter Sofia. You inspire me each and every day, reminding me to always keep laughing… and growing. Thank you for all your encouragement and support (and your patience).

To all my clients over the years, each of you has always been deeply committed to your evolution and growth. Thank you for entrusting me with your stories of triumph and challenge and allowing me to guide your personal and professional journey.

I also want to thank the various organizations and individuals who have invited me to speak and train at their events. Thank you for allowing me to share my insights with your audiences. The feedback and perspectives I've received from attendees have provided rich, real-life context to the leadership concepts discussed in this book.

I am deeply grateful to Practical Inspiration Publishing, especially to Alison Jones and her skilled team, for their indispensable role in bringing this book to life. Thank you so much for taking me on as an author and believing in the contribution I wanted to make to the literature. Your expertise and support have been crucial throughout the publishing process.

Lastly, thank you to you, the reader, who has chosen to embark on this journey with me through these pages. Your engagement and interest in this work are vital to its (and my) journey. I hope the insights, experiences, and tools shared here will resonate with you and aid in your leadership path. Thank you so much for purchasing a copy of this book and committing to your growth. Keep evolving.

# About the Author

Dr. Samantha Madhosingh is an international speaker, leadership consultant, executive coach, and psychologist, who has dedicated her career over the past two decades to assisting leaders and teams with discovering their full potential and optimizing their productivity, performance, and progress without burning out. She is committed to helping leaders and teams work together better because healthy work cultures require exceptional leaders and happy, engaged employees.

Dr. Samantha has published many articles and book chapters on emotional intelligence, leadership, and personal development topics. Her work has been featured in prominent publications like Forbes, Entrepreneur, CEO World Magazine, LifeHack, BlackEnterprise, and The Daily Telegraph. Dr. Samantha has also appeared on tv media outlets in the US, including CW, FOX, NBC, and CBS.

Dr. Samantha is currently based in London, England and continues to speak, train, coach, and consult internationally.

Website: askdrsamantha.com
LinkedIn: www.linkedin.com/in/drsmadhosingh
Facebook: www.facebook.com/drsmadhosingh
Twitter/X: twitter.com/drsmadhosingh
Instagram: www.instagram.com/drsmadhosingh

# Index

1% For the Planet 56

accountability 50–51, 159
actions 5–10, 23, 25, 88
active listening 78–79, 97, 105–107,
    109, 129–130
adaptability 24–25
adaptation 74
affirmations 106
amygdala 32
assertiveness 104–105
attention 143
attention deficit hyperactivity
    disorder (ADHD) 73, 74
authenticity 10
autism 73, 74, 125

Baby Boomers 94–95
behavior 97
belief 13, 29, 34
  and leadership 35–37
  unconscious biases 34–35
biases 34–35, 81–82, 94–96,
    131–132, 157
Blanchard, Kenneth H. xi–xiv
blind spots 18–19

body, assessment of 21–23
body language 77–78, 92, 101–103
brain function 30–34
Branson, Richard 74–75, 91
breathing 33–34
Brown, Brené 71, 77
burnout 141–143, 167, 169

care 107
change for yourself 49–50
  accountability 50–51
  embrace the discomfort 42–43
  your commitment muscle 52–53
Chopra, Deepak 25
Chouinard, Yvon 55–56
Cirillo, Francesco 63–64
civility 86–87
clubs 162
coaching 163, 164, 165
  for better leadership 166–167
  communication skills 169
  reflection with curiosity 168
  risk-taking and confidence 168
  self-awareness 168
  work-life balance 169
cognitive scripts 31

color coding 64
comfort zone 131
commitment 47–50, 56
  and accountability 50–51
  applying the learning 66–67
  building trust 54
  FOCUS 59–60
  to growth 177–180
  motivation 53–54
  muscle 52–53
  SMART goals 56–59
  time management 62–66
communication 87–88, 91–93
  applying the learning 115–116
  challenges 93
  difficult conversations 107–109
  effective communication 97–103
  effective feedback 111–112
  encouraging dialogue 109
  giving/receiving feedback
    109–112
  maladaptive habits 93–97
  preparation 108
  setting 108
  showing you care 107
  skills 169
  storytelling 112–115
  timeliness 108
  tone 108–109
  *see also* body language
communication styles 103
  active listening 78–79, 97,
    105–107, 109, 129–130
  aggressive 104
  assertive 104–105
  manipulative 104
  nonverbal cues 77–78, 99–103,
    105
  passive/aggressive 104
  passive/submissive 103–104
community 162

compassion 118, 119, 122
compassionate command 117–119
  applying the learning 133–134
  building empathy skills 125–133
  empathic leadership 121–124
  empathy 119–121
  empathy for self and others
    124–125
conclusion 185–186
confidence 168
conflict resolution 12
connection 71–73
consensus 85–86
consistency 48–49
  applying the learning 66–67
  building trust 54–55, 56
  FOCUS 59–60
  SMART goals 56–61
  time management 62–66
consultation 85–86
Corcoran, Barbara 75
Cornell University 25
Covey, Stephen R. 98
  *The 7 Habits of Highly Effective*
    *People* 65
cultivating the whole leader xiii–xiv
Cunningham, James 57
curiosity 18, 87, 127–128, 168

Dalai Lama 137
dependency 85–86
dialogue 97, 109
diet 145–146
difficult conversations 107–109
difficult people 85–87
difficult situations 158–159
disagreement 129
Doran, George 57
Dweck, Carol: *Mindset* 178
dyslexia 73
dyspraxia 73

effective communication xiii–xiv,
    97–98
  body language 101–103
  tone of voice 99–100, 102
  what you say 98–99
Eisenhower Matrix 64–65
emotion 17–18, 55, 97, 102,
    171–172, 180–181
Emotion Vocabulary xiv, 197–198
emotional intelligence (EI)
    10–11, 20, 25, 72, 76, 83–85,
    120–121
emotional reactions and behavior
    21
  assess your body 21–23
  focus on adaptability 24–25
  think before you act 23
emotional self-control 20–21
emotions 5
empathy 117–119
  key elements 123–124
  and kindness 122
  leadership 121–124
  science behind 119–121
  skill 121–122
  in the workplace 122–123
  for yourself and others 124–125
empathy skills 125–126
  active listening 129–130
  curiosity 127–128
  empathic listening 79–80, 98
  engage in disagreement 129
  feelings of others 128
  identify your biases 131–132
  outside your comfort zone 131
  read widely 130
  start with you 126
  vulnerability 132–133
Empire Strikes Back, The 29–30, 31
energy management 140–141
exercise 146

exercises 191–196
eye contact 102, 103, 105, 106

facial expressions 77, 78, 92, 101,
    103, 106
feedback 12, 19, 25, 86, 95,
    109–111
  effective feedback 111–112
feelings 5–10, 128
fight-flight-freeze response 32–33
flexibility 74
FOCUS 59–60
foundations of the self xii–xiii,
    197–198
  rewriting the script 29–46
  self-discovery 3–27

Gallup report 110
Gen X, Gen Z 94–95
generalizations 94, 95
gestures 77–78, 101–102
goals see SMART goals
Goleman, Daniel : Emotional
    Intelligence 10–11, 72, 82,
    121, 123–124
gratitude 147
Green Peak Partners 25
growth, commitment to 177–180
  see also sustained growth
Gunn, Tim 155

Haiti earthquakes 117
Hebb, Donald 30
help from others 151
holistic leadership: self-care
    139–140
humor 150

"I don't have time" conundrum
    144–145
identity 13

inclusion 76
insights and action 25
instructions 96–97
Interact/Harris survey 93
internal dialogue 23
International Global Leadership
        Forecast 2021 169
IQ (intelligence quotient) 11
Itani, Omar 56

John, Daymond 75
Jung, Carl 107

Kamprad, Ingvar 75
kindness 38, 122
King, Billie Jean 3

leadership xi–xiv, 71–72, 98, 122
    and belief 35–37
    coaching for 166–167
    empathy 121–124
    see also support system
learning commitment 66–67
listening 78–79, 92, 96
    active listening 78–79, 97,
            105–107, 129–130
    deep listening 98
    empathic listening 79–80, 98
long-term goals 181–182

maladaptive habits 93–94
management 85
manners 87
Mehrabian, Albert 77, 92, 98,
        99–100, 101
mentoring 163, 164, 165
Merriam-Webster Dictionary 91
Millennials 94–95
Miller, Arthur 57
mindfulness 18, 38–39
mindset 29, 172, 178–179
    fixed mindset 179

growth mindset 179–180
mixed signals 87
morale 20
motivation 53–54
Musk, Elon 75

Neeleman, David 75
networking 88, 162
neurodiversity 73–76, 125
neuroplasticity 31
neurotypical brains 73
new things 150
nonverbal cues 77–78, 99–103, 105
notes 187–190

Obama, Barack 117
Ong, Simon Alexander: Energize
        140–141
openness 87
organizational awareness 82–83
organizational culture 20

Patagonia 55–56
personality traits 85, 96
planning 60–61
Pomodoro Technique 63–64
positive relationships 87–88
posture 101–102
problem-solving 84
Proctor, Bob 50
Project Medishare 117–118

reading 130
recognition 111–112
reflection 111, 168
relationship management 83–85
    action 88
    applying the learning 88–89
    communication 98
    difficult people 85–87
    positive relationships 87–88
relationship mastery xiii

resilience 84, 171–173, 178
  applying the learning 184
  bouncing back 173–176
  commitment to growth 177–180
  improving resilience 180–183
  low resilience 176–177
respect 84
results 5–10
risk-taking 168
Rogers, Fred 118
routine 152–153

Samueli Integrative Health
      Programs 142
Schwab, Charles 75
"second thought" strategy 81–82
self-awareness 3–5, 10–11, 21, 25,
      72, 75–76, 83
  big picture 16–17
  blind spots 18–19
  and coaching 168
  the core of 10–11
  curiosity 18
  empathy 124–125
  hacking your self-awareness
      15–19, 96
  lack of 11–12
  patterns of thought and emotion
      17–18
self-care 137–138, 182
  boundaries 138
  and burnout 141–143
  daily self-care 139–140
  energy management 140–141
  for holistic leadership 139–140
  "I don't have time" 144–145
  pay attention! 143
  routine 152–153
  stress triggers 143–144
  toolkit 148–149
self-care: basics
  eat a healthy diet 145–146

  exercise 146
  practice gratitude 147
  sleep 146–147
self-care: more options 149
  ask for help 151
  embrace humor 150
  more! 151–152
  self-reflection tool 151
  try out new things 150
self-care toolkit 148–149
self-discovery 3–5
  applying the learning 26–27
  awareness and control 3–19
  emotional reactions and behavior
      21–25
  exercises 27
  insights and action 25
  thoughts feelings actions results
      5–10
self-empathy 124–125
self-empowerment 168
self-esteem 13
self-examination 81
self-management 19–21
  emotional reactions and behavior
      21–25
self-reflection tool 151
self-regulation 83
self-sabotage 12–15, 37–38
self-talk 23, 41–42, 181
Silent Generation 94–95
sleep 146–147
SMART goals 56–59
  planning 60–61
social awareness 72, 76–77, 83
  action 88
  active listening 78–79
  applying the learning 88–89
  body language 77–78
  challenge your biases 81–82
  empathic listening 79–80
  the whole picture 80

sponsoring 163, 165
Spring Health 141–142
stay the course 47–49
  change for yourself 49–53
  commitment 47–48, 49–50
  consistency 48–49
  motivation 53–54
stereotypes 81, 94–95
stigma 159–161
storytelling 112–113
  key elements 114–115
  skills 113–114
stress triggers (stressors) 143–144
support system 155–157, 183
  applying the learning 170
  coaching 163, 164, 165, 166–169
  mentoring 163, 164, 165
  sponsoring 163, 165
  which to choose? 165–166
support system benefits 157–158
  accountability 159
  difficult situations 158–159
  outside perspective 158
  overcoming stigma 159–161
support system: building up a base
      161–162
  club or community group 162
  introduce yourself to others 163
  networking at work 162
sustained growth 137–138
  applying the learning 153
  basics 145–148
  energy management 140–141
  "I don't have time" conundrum
      144–145
  more options 149–152
  pay attention! 143
  self-care 137–138
  self-care and burnout 141–143
  self-care for holistic leadership
      139–140
  stress triggers 143–144

Tallinn University 168
team dynamics 167
Teams Instant Message 96
think before you act 23
thoughts 5–10, 17–18
time blocking 64
time management 62–64
  color coding 64
  difficult conversations 108
  "I don't have time" conundrum
      144–145
  Pomodoro Technique 63–64
  time blocking 64
  Time Management Matrix 65–66
timeliness 108
timing 92
tone
  of conversation 108–109
  of voice 99–100, 102
Tourette's syndrome 73
toxic positivity 172
trust 11, 54–56, 98, 122

uncertainty 182–183
unconscious biases 34–35
understanding others
  applying the learning 88–89
  civility 86–87
  connection 71–73
  difficult people 85–87
  neurodiverse and nuerotypical
      brains 73–76
  organizational awareness 82–83
  positive relationships 87–88
  relationship management 83–85
  social awareness skills 76–82
unhelpful habits 93–94
University of Miami School of
      Medicine 117
unlearning process 29–30
  applying the learning 45
  belief 34–37

brain function 30–34
exercises 46
mindfulness 18, 38–39
self-sabotage 12–15, 37–38
unlearning process: practical
    strategies 39–40
embrace discomfort of change
    42–43
embrace the journey 40–41
focus on the new 44
language in self-talk 41–42
learn from others 44
prioritize importance 43–44

vulnerability 132–133

Winfrey, Oprah 121, 142–143
work-life balance 169

workplace relationships 83–85
action 88
applying the learning 88–89
civility 86–87
compassion 122
difficult people 85–87
empathy 122–123
kindness 122
positive relationships 87–88
relationship management 83–85
World Health Organization 141

## A quick word from Practical Inspiration Publishing...

We hope you found this book both practical and inspiring – that's what we aim for with every book we publish.

We publish titles on topics ranging from leadership, entrepreneurship, HR and marketing to self-development and wellbeing.

Find details of all our books at: www.practicalinspiration.com

 **Did you know...**

We can offer discounts on bulk sales of all our titles – ideal if you want to use them for training purposes, corporate giveaways or simply because you feel these ideas deserve to be shared with your network.

We can even produce bespoke versions of our books, for example with your organization's logo and/or a tailored foreword.

To discuss further, contact us on info@practicalinspiration.com.

 **Got an idea for a business book?**

We may be able to help. Find out more about publishing in partnership with us at: bit.ly/PIpublishing.

*Follow us on social media...*

🐦 @PIPTalking

📷 @pip_talking

f @practicalinspiration

♪ @piptalking

in Practical Inspiration Publishing

www.ingramcontent.com/pod-product-compliance
Lightning Source LLC
Jackson TN
JSHW011441280125

77976JS00009B/77